Series

Work Out

Accounting

'A' Level

The titles in this series

MACMILLAN
WORK OUT
SERIES

Work Out

Accounting

'A' Level

P. Stevens

and

B. Kriefman

MACMILLAN

First published 1988

Published by
MACMILLAN EDUCATION LTD
Houndmills, Basingstoke, Hampshire RG21 2XS
and London
Companies and representatives
throughout the world

Printed in Great Britain by
The Bath Press Ltd, Avon

British Library Cataloguing in Publication Data
Stevens, P.
Work out accounting: 'A' Level. — (Macmillan
work out series).
1. Accounting — Examinations, questions, etc.
I. Title   II. Kriefman, B.
657'.076   HF5661
ISBN 0-333-45124-4
ISBN 0-333-45125-2 Export

Contents

Acknowledgements

The University of London Entrance and School Examinations Council accepts no responsibility whatsoever for the accuracy or method in the answers given in this book to actual questions set by the London Board.

Acknowledgement is made to the Southern Universities' Joint Board for School Examinations for permission to use questions taken from their past papers but the Board is in no way responsible for answers that may be provided and they are solely the responsibility of the authors.

The Associated Examining Board, the University of Oxford Delegacy of Local Examinations, the Northern Ireland Schools Examination Council and the Scottish Examination Board wish to point out that worked examples included in the text are entirely the responsibility of the author and have neither been provided nor approved by the Board.

Examination Boards for Advanced Level

Syllabuses and past examination papers can be obtained from:

The Associated Examining Board (AEB)
Stag Hill House
Guildford
Surrey GU2 5XJ

University of Cambridge Local Examinations Syndicate (UCLES)
Syndicate Buildings
Hills Road
Cambridge CB1 2EU

Joint Matriculation Board (JMB)
78 Park Road
Altrincham
Cheshire WA14 5QQ

University of London School Examinations Board (L)
University of London Publications Office
52 Gordon Square
London WC1E 6EE

University of Oxford (OLE)
Delegacy of Local Examinations
Ewert Place
Summertown
Oxford OX2 7BZ

Oxford and Cambridge Schools Examination Board (O&C)
10 Trumpington Street
Cambridge CB2 1QB

Scottish Examination Board (SEB)
Robert Gibson & Sons (Glasgow) Ltd
17 Fitzroy Place
Glasgow G3 7SF

Southern Universities' Joint Board (SUJB)
Cotham Road
Bristol BS6 6DD

Welsh Joint Education Committee (WJEC)
245 Western Avenue
Cardiff CF5 2YX

Northern Ireland Schools Examination Council (NISEC)
Examinations Office
Beechill House
Beechill Road
Belfast BT8 4RS

Introduction

How to Use this Book

This book makes the assumption that you have already mastered the subject at 'O' level and if this is not so you may find it necessary to refer back to your 'O' level textbook in order to understand some of the topics in this book. If you are not in possession of an appropriate 'O' level textbook then there is a suitable book in the 'O' level Work Out series. The 'A' level papers include many questions on topics examined at 'O' level but usually will introduce additional areas and involve far more calculations than at 'O' level.

In using this book you are recommended to read each chapter, making sure you understand the technique being explained before proceeding to the next point. You should then study the worked examples and solutions, ensuring that you fully understand how the solutions have been arrived at, and why.

Revision

Before you start to revise, find out exactly which syllabus you are following and obtain a copy of it. The book contains many questions from the most recent examination papers of various examination boards. However, having worked through these, you may wish to obtain copies of past papers from your own examination board. Certainly the best way to check your revision progress in Accounting is to work carefully through as many typical questions as you possibly can. Take a topic at a time, make certain that you understand fully the key points of theory and then attempt a range of questions.

The Examination

In practical accounting examinations it is vital that you allocate the time you spend on each question according to the number of marks awarded for the question. Calculate how long you can afford to spend on each question and do not spend more time on it.

1 Accounting Concepts

1.1 Introduction

Although you may not have been aware of it, you have already been applying certain accounting concepts when you were preparing accounting statements in your earlier studies. Examples of this are in valuation of stock and depreciation of fixed assets. The method of dealing with these operations has arisen from generally accepted accounting concepts. One further example is the differentiation between capital and revenue expenditure, where such expenses as rent and wages have been treated as revenue expenditures and have been taken account of in the calculation of the net profit. Capital expenditures – for example, fixtures – have been treated as an asset and have not been taken account of in the profit calculation (except by way of depreciation).

We shall now consider in turn some accounting concepts, all of which are applied in the preparation of accounting statements. The first two are very basic and therefore, while universally accepted, are taken for granted. The third concept, of materiality, is also taken for granted. The last four are embodied in a document called Statement of Standard Accounting Practice (SSAP) No. 2. Chapter 5 explains what these standards are and looks at them in greater depth.

1.2 Business entity concept

Your first studies of accounting will have made it clear that what we are doing is keeping the books or accounts of a business and not the owner's personal books. For this reason we consider the business separately from its owner and record only those transactions which affect the business. Thus, we ignore private transactions, and also the owner's personal assets and liabilities.

1.3 Money measurement concept

Accounting is about recording things which can be measured in money terms. For example, assets are recorded at their cost in money terms to the business. For the same reason we ignore any assets of the business which it has not paid for in money terms – for example, goodwill that the business may have built up, either with its customers or with its employees. Similarly, in stating liabilities, we are concerned with the monetary value of those liabilities.

1.4 Materiality concept

The materiality concept recognises that if we tried to be absolutely precise about everything, it would cost the business considerable time and expense. Stock valuation and depreciation are good examples of where absolute precision, even if it were possible, would involve tremendous time, trouble and expense.

Where the amount of any possible error would have an immaterial effect on the accounting statements, it is both reasonable and acceptable to use best approximation to actual value.

1.5 Going concern concept

Accounting statements are prepared on the basis that the business will continue to operate as it has been, for the foreseeable future. It therefore assumes that the business is not likely to terminate the whole or part of those operations in the near future.

The treatment of fixed assets can be considered under this concept. Fixed assets are depreciated with the object of writing off the cost (less residual value) over their useful life. It is irrelevant that the asset could not be sold for its balance sheet value (that is to say, we ignore a lower realisable value for fixed assets). Similarly, we would not be interested in the fact that it would cost us substantially more to replace the asset.

1.6 Accruals or matching concept

Expenses should be matched against the revenues which are earned as a result of those costs. This is why we accrue for expenses incurred during an accounting period, even though we have not paid for them — for example, wages due but unpaid. Similarly, where the revenue has not yet been earned, we carry forward the associated or related costs — for example, in the stock evaluation.

1.7 Consistency concept

Where there are alternative methods of accounting, such as with depreciation and stock valuation, it is necessary to apply consistent treatment in every accounting period.

1.8 Prudence concept

Profits should not be recognised until they are realised, which is taken to mean when goods are sold, for example. Also, all expenses and losses should be accrued when they become apparent; this in *some* cases can mean altering accounts before they have been signed by the directors.

You should realise that the concept is not designed to enable deliberate understatement of profits and the creation of hidden reserves. Rather it is designed to err on the prudent side where there is genuine doubt surrounding the value of an asset or liability. This means that assets should be understated rather than overstated, and liabilities overstated rather than understated.

1.9 Worked examples

Example 1.1

Two of the Concepts of Accounting are 'Matching' and the 'Going Concern' concept. Explain fully what these concepts are and why they are so important in preparing accounts.

(OLE)

Solution 1.1

For explanations refer to the text.

The importance of matching is to ensure that the profit is a true and fair figure and to ensure that profits (or losses) do not fluctuate violently from year to year for reasons of accounting treatment rather than trading activity. For example, consider what would happen to profits if in Year 1 we omitted to accrue for a substantial amount of wages for no reason other than the fact that we had not yet paid our labour force. Year 1's profit would be unduly high, since it would take no account of this cost, whereas Year 2's profit would be unduly low, since it would bear the cost but with no related revenue.

The importance of the going concern concept can also be attributed to the above reasons. If fixed assets were adjusted to their realisable value each year, then each year's profits would not reflect a depreciation charge which spreads the costs of the assets in a fair manner. Rather profits would reflect realisable values of fixed assets bearing little relevance to the trading activities of the business for that year.

Example 1.2

With one month of the financial year remaining, indications are that Stainer plc will return a profit figure substantially lower than that earned in previous years. In addition, the company's bank overdraft has increased considerably and is now close to the limit set by the bank. The managing director, after discussion with other directors, is considering the following three proposals.

(1) To include both profit and interest on a substantial three year credit sale in this year's revenue accounts. Previous accounting policy has been to apportion both profit and interest over the length of the credit agreement.
(2) To delay a credit payment to a major supplier until the final settlement date, which occurs early in the next financial year, despite an offer of substantial cash discount if early payment is received.
(3) To sell for £50,000 cash an item of plant and machinery which is surplus to requirements. The machine cost £250,000 when purchased four years ago and has been depreciated by £100,000.

REQUIRED

    (a) Outline the effect of **each** of the three proposals on both the cash situation and projected profit of the company. [*12 marks*]
    (b) Advise the managing director as to the accounting principles involved in proposals (1) **and** (3) above. [*10 marks*]

(AEB)

Solution 1.2

(a) (1) The cash situation would be unaffected. Profit would be substantially higher, since it would reflect the total profit and interest on the credit sale, as opposed to only one-third (or less) thereof.
    (2) The overdraft would be reduced and trade creditors would remain at the higher level. Profit would be reduced by the amount of the cash discount.
    (3) The overdraft would be reduced by £50,000. The profit would be reduced by a loss or disposal of fixed assets of £100,000.
(b) (1) The company should be consistent in the application of accounting bases and continue to recognise profits and interest over the length of the agreement. To recognise all of the interest element in the current year would also be contrary to the matching concept, since the interest income does

not relate to that year and the associated financing costs would not be reported in that year. (Refer to note at end concerning profit.)

(2) The loss on the sale of the machinery would have to be recognised, since it would be realised. Even if it were not sold, Stainer plc would need to convince its auditors that the machinery is only temporarily surplus to requirements and that it would, in the foreseeable future, be put to profitable use by the company. If it were unable to convince them of this they would need to recognise the diminutions in value in its accounts even if it were not sold.

Note: In regard to b(1) and the profit element, Statement of Standard Accounting Practice (SSAP) 21, 'Accounting for leases and hire purchase contracts', requires the profit to be recognised in the year of the sale. The company would therefore need to amend its accounting policies to reflect this. A knowledge of this SSAP is outside the scope of most 'A'-level syllabuses.

Example 1.3

Choose four different ways of calculating or allocating depreciation and explain the difference between them. In each case state the type of asset for which it might be used, giving a reason.

Solution 1.3

(1) *Straight line method*   This method apportions the cost (less residual value) equally over the estimated life of the asset; in other words, it calculates depreciation as a fixed and equal amount of cost for each year. It is the most commonly used method, and is appropriate for most types of fixed asset — for example, plant and machinery.

(2) *Reducing balance method*   This method calculates depreciation as a fraction of the previous year's net book value. Thus, the depreciation charge is comparatively high in the early years but quickly becomes comparatively low. It is therefore appropriate where the early years in the life of an asset enjoy its most efficient use and when it is also incurring comparatively low repair and maintenance charges. For this reason it might be appropriate for such assets as motor vehicles.

(3) *Machine hour method*   This method is used where we can estimate the life of an item of machinery in terms of the hours of use that we can expect from it. The depreciation charge would be based on the hours of use as a fraction of its total expected hours of use throughout its life. It is therefore appropriate for any item of plant where the major cause of its loss in value is through use, rather than time, and this usage can be quantified in terms of hours reasonably accurately.

(4) *Revaluation method*   The depreciation charge is calculated by adding purchases of new assets to the opening value for assets of that type and deducting from this the closing value of these assets. It is appropriate for such items as small tools (manufacturing company) or cutlery (hotel or restaurant) where there are several small items of low but lasting value.

Example 1.4

Explain with two examples of each the difference between revenue expenditure and capital expenditure. Why is the distinction between the two important in preparing final accounts and balance sheets?

Solution 1.4

Revenue expenditure such as rent and wages is taken account of in calculating the profit of the business. Capital expenditure is expenditure on fixed assets such as buildings and machinery, and is not taken account of in calculating profit (except by way of depreciation). The distinction is important, therefore, since the treatment of revenue expenditure as capital expenditure will show an unfairly high profit figure and, conversely, the treatment of capital expenditure as revenue expenditure will show an unfairly low profit figure.

1.10 Further exercises

Question 1.1

Name four fundamental accounting concepts and explain what is meant by two of them.
(OLE)

Answer 1.1

Refer to the text.

Question 1.2

What is the purpose of depreciation? What factors should be taken into account when considering the annual charge for the depreciation of an asset?
(OLE)

Answer 1.2

Refer to the text and Example 1.3.

Question 1.3

What is the relationship between provision for depreciation and the replacement of an asset.
(OLE)

Answer 1.3

Refer to the text. Also, the object of depreciation is *not* to provide for its eventual replacement. Any setting aside for replacement of assets is a transfer to reserves (an appropriation of profit), not a provision (charge against profits).

2 Partnership Accounts

2.1 Introduction

Examination questions on the topic of partnership accounts, in particular, will be set to examine your understanding of other accounting areas. These will include subjects such as year-end adjustments and forecasts which you studied at 'O' level. You should study the worked examples very carefully to ensure that you have a thorough grasp of these 'O' level topics. It may be necessary for you to go back to your 'O' level book to revise these areas.

2.2 The partnership agreement

It is advisable for the partners to draw up an agreement covering the following areas:

  (i) *Capital*   How much each should contribute and leave in the business.

 (ii) *Profit sharing*   One partner may be entitled to a greater share of the profits because he has more experience or is doing a greater share of the work.

(iii) *Salaries*   One or more partners may be entitled to a salary because of the work they are performing.

(iv) *Interest on capital*   This might be appropriate where one or more partners is contributing a materially greater sum than others.

 (v) *Drawings*   The agreement should cover the amount of profits that may be withdrawn and may further discourage drawings by charging interest on them.

Any points not covered in the partnership agreement are decided by reference to the Partnership Act 1890, which states:

  (i) Profits are shared equally.

 (ii) There are no partnership salaries.

(iii) Partners shall receive no interest on capital but should receive 5 per cent interest per annum on any loans to the business.

2.3 Admission of new partner

When a new partner is about to be admitted, the existing partners will give consideration to revaluing assets – in particular, goodwill. In order to revalue assets, we debit the asset account with the increase in value of that asset and credit the partners' capital accounts according to their profit-sharing ratios. Similarly, if we want to recognise the value of goodwill built up by the existing partners, we debit a goodwill account and credit the existing partners' capital accounts according to their profit-sharing ratios.

Often the partners will decide that they do not want the value of goodwill appearing on the balance sheet. This is due to the uncertain value and nature of such an asset. In order to eliminate goodwill, we must credit the goodwill account and debit the partners' capital accounts (including the new partner) according to their new profit-sharing ratios.

2.4 Realisation accounts

When a partnership ceases, it becomes necessary to close the books of account and record what happens to the assets and liabilities of the partnership.

The first step is to transfer the assets of the partnership from the asset accounts to a realisation account. We do this by debiting the realisation account and crediting the appropriate asset account. If these assets are sold for cash, we debit cash or bank with the proceeds and credit the realisation account. If the assets are taken over by one of the partners, we debit the partner's capital account and credit the realisation account with the agreed value for that asset.

The next stage is to pay any liabilities of the partnership (debit the liability account and credit cash or bank). There will usually be, additionally, realisation costs involved; these are debited to the realisation account.

The balance on the realisation account will now represent the profit or loss on winding up the partnership. This profit or loss is apportioned to the partners according to their profit-sharing ratios and is transferred to their current accounts.

The balances on the partners' current accounts are then transferred to their capital accounts. At this stage the only accounts that remain open are capital accounts and cash or bank. The books are finally closed by paying the partners the balance on their capital accounts or receiving from them the amounts due where they show a debit balance.

In the event of a partner's capital accounting showing a debit balance and his being unable to pay the amount due, there is an important legal point which should be noted. This is the Garner vs Murray 1904 rule, which states that, in the event of a partner being unable to pay the debit balance on his capital account, it must be shared by the other partners in proportion to their last agreed capitals.

2.5 Worked examples

Example 2.1

Misfit and Wartz are in partnership. At 31 December 1984 they agree that their assets are worth:

	£
Premises	200,000
Fixtures	80,000
Motor vehicles	60,000
Stock	20,000
Debtors	8,200
Bank	1,200
Cash	300

At the same date they have creditors of 5,700

During the year ending 31 December 1985 the following transactions took place:

1. On 1 July 1985 Misfit loaned the partnership £20,000 for ten years.
2. At the same date, Wartz increased his capital by £36,000 to make it equal to Misfit's.
3. Cash sales for the year were £300,000.
4. £490,200 was paid into the bank during the year.
5. Expenses paid in cash during the year were £2,400.

6. Expenses paid by cheque during the year were:

   (i) wages £56,000;

   (ii) lighting and heating and rates £9,700;

   (iii) motor vehicle expenses £18,300;

   (iv) carriage on purchases £3,400;

   (v) other expenses £18,800.

7. Some small items of goods for resale were purchased and paid for out of the cash £10,000.

8. Goods which cost £1,200 had been returned to credit suppliers.

9. £288,720 was paid to creditors during the year. 10% cash discount had been deducted from all payments.

10. No discounts were allowed to debtors, but £200 had been written off as bad.

11. One of the vehicles is used occasionally by Misfit's wife. The cost of this usage (included in the motor vehicle expenses) is estimated to be £3,400; this to be charged to Misfit.

12. Both partners had taken goods from the business during the year valued at cost. These were estimated at:

Misfit   £2,800;   Wartz   £1,900.

13. At 31 December 1985, fixtures and motor vehicles were valued at £72,000 and £60,341, respectively, stocks were valued at £22,500, debtors owed £5,500 and creditors were owed £6,400.

14. A small amount of cash is kept in the business from cash sales for paying expenses, and at 31 December, 1985, there is £500 not paid into the bank.

15. On 1 June 1985 a small van with a book value of £750 was sold for £900 and replaced by a new one at a cost of £7,800. The difference was paid by cheque.

16. During the year the partners had withdrawn from the bank for their own use: Misfit £3,840; Wartz £18,200.

17. Watkinson is the general manager for the partnership, and apart from his wages he is entitled to a bonus of 10% of the net profit of the business calculated after charging this bonus. The bonus will be paid on 1 February 1986.

18. Interest is allowed on partnership capital of 5% per annum and Wartz is allowed a salary of £15,000 per annum. Interest is charged on these drawings, but apart from these no other agreements have been made.

19. The interest on drawings for the year has been calculated at Misfit £300 and Wartz £550.

You are required to prepare:

(a) the Trading and Profit and Loss account of the partnership for the year ended 31 December 1985,

(b) the partners' current accounts and

(c) the Balance Sheet at 31 December 1985.

[*40*]

(OLE)

8

Solution 2.1

(a) Misfit and Wartz: Trading and profit and loss account for year ended
31 December 1985

	£	£	£
Sales [Working 2]			444,300
less Cost of sales			
Stock 1 January 1985		20,000	
Purchases [Working 3]	332,700		
add Carriage	3,400		
	336,100		
less Returns	1,200		
	334,900		
less Stock withdrawn	4,700	330,200	
		350,200	
less Stock 31 December 1985		22,500	
Cost of sales			327,700
Gross profit			116,600
add Discounts received			32,080
Profit on sale of motor van			150
			148,830
less Wages		56,000	
Lighting and heating		9,700	
Motor vehicle expenses [£18,300 − £3,400]		14,900	
Other expenses [£18,800 + £2,400]		21,200	
Depreciation of fixtures [Working 4]		8,000	
Depreciation of motor vehicles [Working 4]		6,709	
Bad debts		200	
Loan interest		500	
Manager's bonus		2,875	120,084
Net profit			28,746

Misfit and Wartz: Profit and loss appropriation account for year ended
31 December 1985

		£	£
Net profit			28,746
add Interest on drawings Misfit		300	
Wartz		550	850
			29,596
less Interest on capital [Working 6]	Misfit	10,000	
	Wartz	9,100	19,100
			10,496
less Salary Wartz			15,000
			(4,504)
Residual loss	Misfit (half)		2,252
	Wartz (half)		2,252	(4,504)

9

(b)

Partners' current accounts

		Misfit £	Wartz £			Misfit £	Wartz £
Dec. 31	Drawings (stock)	2,800	1,900	Dec. 31 Profit and loss appropriation (interest)		10,000	9,100
	Motor vehicle usage	3,400		Profit and loss appropriation (salary)			15,000
	Drawings (bank)	3,840	18,200	Loan interest		500	
	Interest on drawings	300	550				
	Profit and loss appropriation	2,252	2,252				
	Balance c/d	—	1,198	Balance c/d		2,092	—
		12,592	24,100			12,592	24,100

(c)

Misfit and Wartz: Balance Sheet as at 31 December 1985

	£	£	£
Fixed assets			
Premises			200,000
Fixtures			72,000
Motor vehicles			60,341
			332,341
Current assets			
Stock		22,500	
Debtors		5,500	
Bank		67,540	
Cash		500	
		96,040	
less Current liabilities			
Creditors	6,400		
Manager's bonus	2,875	9,275	
Working capital			86,765
Net assets			419,106
Capital accounts Misfit			200,000
Wartz			200,000
			400,000
Current accounts Misfit		(2,092)	
Wartz		1,198	(894)
			399,106
Loan Misfit			20,000
			£419,106

WORKING 1: Cash book

		Cash £	Bank £			Cash £	Bank £
Jan. 1	Balance b/d	300	1,200	Dec. 31	Bank*	287,400	
July 1	Loan (Misfit)		20,000		Expenses	2,400	
July 1	Capital (Wartz)		36,000		Wages		56,000
Dec. 31	Sales	300,000			Lighting and heating		9,700
	Cash		287,400		Motor vehicle expenses		18,300
	Debtors*		146,800		Carriage		3,400
					Other		18,800
					Purchases	10,000	
					Creditors		288,720
					Motor van		6,900
					Drawings Misfit		3,840
					Wartz		18,200
					Balance c/d	500	67,540*
		300,300	491,400			300,300	491,400

*These are balancing figures.

WORKING 2: Sales

	£
Receipts from debtors	146,800
add Owing at 31 December 1985	5,500
add Bad debt written off	200
	152,500
less Owing at 1 January 1985	8,200
	144,300
Cash sales	300,000
	444,300

WORKING 3: Purchases

	£
Paid to creditors	288,720
add Back discounts (10/90)	32,080
	320,800
add Owing at 31 December 1985	6,400
	327,200
less Owing at 1 January 1985	5,700
	321,500
add Cash purchases	10,000
Returns	1,200
	332,700

WORKING 4: Depreciation

	Motor vehicles £	Fixtures £
Value at 1 January 1985	60,000	80,000
add Purchase	7,800	
	67,800	
less Book value of sale	750	
	67,050	
less Value at 31 December 1985	60,341	72,000
	6,709	8,000

WORKING 5: Net profit before charging bonus

	£
Net profit before charging bonus	86,721
10/110 thereof	7,884

WORKING 6: Interest on capital

	Misfit £	Wartz £
Opening capital*	200,000	164,000
5% thereof	10,000	8,200
5% × 6/12 × additional capital [£36,000]		900
	10,000	9,100

*Calculated from value of business at 31 December 1984.

Example 2.2

Ken Brown, Peter Green and James White have been in partnership for a number of years, sharing profits and losses 3:2:1, respectively. At 31 December 1984 their Balance Sheet contains the following items:

		£		£
Capital Accounts:	Brown	20,000	Fixed Assets	32,500
	Green	10,000	Debtors	7,000
	White	10,000	Stock	4,200
Current Accounts:	Brown	2,000	Bank	1,500
	Green	500 DR	Creditors	1,200
	White	1,500 DR		
Loan	Smith	4,000		
		44,000		44,000

Green and White both have businesses of their own which they operate separately from the partnership, Green agreeing to absorb some of the business into his own. As he is taking some of the partnership customers into his own business, it is agreed to value the goodwill for these at £3,000. Green is asked to pay only his share of this.

As Green does not require the partnership premises, they are sold for £20,000, and other fixed assets are taken over by Green at an agreed valuation of £12,000. Half the stock is taken by Green at its cost, the remainder being sold for £2,700. Green takes over the debtors after £500 has been written off as bad. The creditors are paid in full.

Half the loan is paid to Smith, who agrees to transfer the other half to Green for payment by him at a later date. The expenses of winding up the partnership were £500.

You are required to prepare the partners' capital and current accounts, the bank account and the realisation account to record the dissolution of the partnership.

[*18 marks*]

Solution 2.2

Realisation account

	£			£
Jan. 1 Fixed assets	32,500	Jan. 1	Goodwill	3,000
Debtors	7,000		Capital Green (stock)	2,100
Stock	4,200		Bank (stock)	2,700
Bank (realisation expenses)	500		Capital Green (debtors)	6,500
Current a/c Brown [$\frac{3}{6}$ × £2,100]	1,050		Bank (premises)	20,000
Green [$\frac{2}{6}$ × £2,100]	700		Capital Green (fixed	
White [$\frac{1}{6}$ × £2,100]	350		assets)	12,000
	46,300			46,300

Capital accounts

	Brown £	Green £	White £			Brown £	Green £	White £
Jan. 1 Goodwill (written off)	1,500	1,000	500	Jan. 1	Balance b/d	20,000	10,000	10,000
Realisation		2,100			Current a/c	3,050	200	
Realisation		6,500			Smith		2,000	
Realisation		12,000						
Current a/c			1,150		Bank		9,400	
Bank	21,550		8,350					
	23,050	21,600	10,000			23,050	21,600	10,000

Current accounts

	Brown £	Green £	White £			Brown £	Green £	White £
Jan. 1 Balance b/d		500	1,500	Jan. 1	Balance b/d	2,000		
					Realisation	1,050	700	350
Capital (balance)	3,050	200			Capital (balance)			1,150
	3,050	700	1,500			3,050	700	1,500

Bank

	£			£
Jan. 1 Balance b/d	1,500	Realisation		500
Realisation a/c	2,700	Creditors		1,200
Realisation a/c	20,000	Smith		2,000
Capital Green	9,400	Capital Brown		21,550
		White		8,350
	33,600			33,600

Example 2.3

(a) What four items would you expect a partnership agreement to contain?
(b) What would happen when preparing the final accounts if the agreement failed to mention these items?

Solution 2.3

(a) Refer to the text. Profit sharing, salaries, interest on capital, drawings.
(b) Refer to the text.

Example 2.4

A and B are in partnership sharing profits and losses in the ratio 3:2. Their last balance sheet as at 31 December 1984 was as follows:

	£	£		£	£
Capital Accounts			Fixed Assets		
A	16,000		Machinery	10,000	
B	12,000		Vehicles	8,000	
		28,000			18,000
Current Accounts			Current Assets		
A	3,000		Stock	30,000	
B	2,000		Debtors	22,000	
		5,000			52,000
Current Liabilities					
Bank overdraft	23,000				
Creditors	14,000				
		37,000			
		70,000			70,000

The partnership has been profitable over many years and although profitability has been maintained, recently the firm has suffered from cash-flow problems. In addition to the cash-flow problems, the partnership needs to reinvest in fixed assets at a cost of £42,000. Profits have been £40,000 per annum over the last three years and it is anticipated that the same level of profit will continue during the present year. Profit accrues evenly throughout the year.

A and B are considering two alternative methods of raising the necessary funds from 1 July 1985:

(1) To purchase the fixed assets on hire purchase over a period of three years. The hire purchase agreement provides for 36 equal instalments of £1,500. (It can be assumed that interest is applied evenly over the three years.) In addition a long-term loan of £30,000 is available from a finance company at 15 per cent interest with only the interest being repayable over the first two years.

(2) To accept into the partnership a new partner C on the following terms from 1 July 1985:
   - That C will bring into the partnership £60,000 cash as capital.
   - That the partners will be entitled to interest at the rate of 15 per cent per year on fixed capital.
   - That A and B will be entitled to a salary of £3,200 per annum and £2,000 per annum, respectively.
   - That the balance of profits and losses will be shared equally between the partners.

(a) A forecast profit and loss appropriation account for the year ending 31 December 1985 assuming that alternative (1) is accepted showing clearly the adjusted net profit figure prior to appropriation. [*8 marks*]

(b) A forecast profit and loss appropriation account for the year ending 31 December 1985 assuming that alternative (2) is accepted. [*12 marks*]

(AEB)

Solution 2.4

(a)

Forecast profit and loss appropriation account of A & B for year ending 31 December 1985

		£	£
Net profit [Working 1]			36,750
apportioned A $\frac{3}{5}$		22,050	
B $\frac{2}{5}$		14,700	36,750

(b)

Forecast profit and loss appropriation account of A & B for year ending 31 December 1985

		Jan/June		July/Dec			
		£	£	£	£	£	£
Net profit			20,000		20,000		40,000
less Interest on capital	A	1,200		1,200		2,400	
	B	900		900		1,800	
	C		2,100	4,500	6,600	4,500	8,700
			17,900		13,400		31,300
less Salary	A			1,600		1,600	
	B			1,000	2,600	1,000	2,600
			17,900		10,800		28,700
Residual profits	A	10,740		3,600		14,340	
	B	7,160		3,600		10,760	
	C		17,900	3,600	10,800	3,600	28,700

WORKING 1

	£	£
Net profits as previous years		40,000
less Interest on HP agreement [$\frac{6}{36} \times$ (£48,000 − £42,000)] =	1,000	
Interest on loan [$\frac{6}{12} \times 15\% \times$ £30,000]	2,250	3,250
		36,750

2.6 Further exercises

Question 2.1

James, Peter and Paul have been in partnership for several years, trading as Goodgame and Co. On 1 January 1982, Peter announces his intention to retire. James and Paul invite John, a young accountant, to join them in partnership. James, Peter and Paul share profits 3:2:1, respectively, and their agreement allows for interest on capitals at 5 per cent per annum.

Peter finally retires on 30 June 1982, and John is admitted into the partnership on 1 July 1982. On Peter's retirement the goodwill of the business is valued at £30,000. Before John is admitted James and Paul agree to revalue the premises to £120,000 and Fittings to £18,000. Because the stock contains several obsolete items it is decided that the value should be reduced by £2,000.

The agreement between James, Paul and John allows for interest on capital at 8 per cent and a partnership salary to John of £8,000 per annum. John is to receive $\frac{1}{4}$ of the profits and James and Paul are to share the remainder equally. John is asked to bring in £5,000 as his share of the goodwill and £5,000 capital. John agrees that he will leave £5,000 of his profit per annum in the business as capital until it equals £25,000. Profits will then be shared equally. Until this time John will not receive interest on his capital.

On the entry of John, Paul agrees to leave his share of the goodwill brought in by John in his Capital account. James is allowed to withdraw his share of this goodwill at any time.

At 31 December 1982 the following trial balance is prepared from the books. No adjustments have been made in the books for any of the items agreed at the time of the change of partnership. The only entries made are that all the payments made by John have been credited to his current account. Peter's share of the goodwill has been paid to him on 30 June 1982, and his capital account has been reduced by the same amount. He has agreed to leave the remainder in the partnership until 1 January 1983.

Trial Balance – Goodgame & Co. at 31 December 1982

	£	£
Capital – James		30,000
Peter		10,000
Paul		23,600
Current account – James		7,500
Peter		5,500
Paul		5,100
John		10,000
Drawings – James	6,400	
Peter	3,200	
Paul	2,000	
Net Trading Profit 31 December 1982		53,760
Freehold premises at cost	60,000	
Motor Vehicles at cost	22,500	
Fixtures and Fittings at cost	14,000	
Stock at 31 December 1982	8,400	
Bank Balance	40,300	
Debtors and Creditors	12,800	10,540
Provision for Depreciation 31 December 1982 Fixtures and Fittings		4,200
Provision for Depreciation Motor Vehicles		10,250
Expenses prepaid and accrued	4,040	3,190
	£173,640	£173,640

NOTES:

1. It can be assumed that profit accrued evenly over the year.
2. Provision for depreciation has been charged on the cost of the Fixture and Fittings and Motor Vehicles at 5 per cent per annum and 10 per cent per annum, respectively.
3. A goodwill account is not to be raised in the books and all adjustments are to be capitalised.

You are required to prepare:

    (i) The Capital and Current accounts of the partners, showing the adjustments necessary on the change of the partnership.

    (ii) The Appropriation account for the year ending 31 December 1982.

    (iii) The Balance Sheet at 31 December 1982.

[40]

(OLE)

Answer 2.1

(i)

Capital a/c James

		£				£
July 1	Goodwill written off [Working 3]	12,500	Jan. 1	Balance b/d		30,000
Dec. 31	Balance c/d	65,425	June 30	Revaluation [Working 1]		32,925
				Goodwill [Working 2]		15,000
		77,925				77,925

Capital a/c Peter

		£				£
June 30	Bank	10,000	Jan. 1	Balance b/d		20,000
Dec. 31	Loan	41,950	June 30	Revaluation [Working 1]		21,950
				Goodwill [Working 2]		10,000
		51,950				51,950

Capital a/c Paul

		£				£
July 1	Goodwill written off [Working 3]	12,500	Jan. 1	Balance b/d		23,600
Dec. 31	Balance c/d	27,075	June 30	Revaluation [Working 1]		10,975
				Goodwill [Working 2]		5,000
		39,575				39,575

Capital a/c John

		£			£
Dec. 31	Balance c/d	10,000	Dec. 31	Current a/c	10,000
		10,000			10,000

Current a/c James

		£			£
Dec. 31	Drawings	6,400	Jan. 1	Balance b/d	7,500
	Balance c/d	24,142		Profit and loss appropriation (interest)	3,367
				Profit and loss appropriation (profit)	19,675
		30,542			30,542

Current a/c Peter

		£			£
Dec. 31	Drawings	3,200	Jan. 1	Balance b/d	5,500
	Loan	11,147		Profit and loss	
				appropriation (interest)	500
				Profit and loss	
				appropriation (profit)	8,347
		———			———
		14,347			14,347

Current a/c Paul

		£			£
Dec. 31	Drawings	2,000	Jan. 1	Balance b/d	5,100
	Balance c/d	16,101		Profit and loss	
				appropriation (interest)	1,673
				Profit and loss	
				appropriation (profit)	11,328
		———			———
		18,101			18,101

Current a/c John

		£			£
Dec. 31	Capital	10,000	July 1	Bank	10,000
	Goodwill	5,000		Profit and loss	
	Balance c/d	3,770		appropriation (sales)	4,000
				Profit and loss	
				appropriation (profit)	4,770
		———			———
		18,770			18,770

(ii)

Goodgame and Co.: appropriation account for year ended 31 December 1982

			Jan./June		July/Dec.		Year
			£	£	£	£	£
Net profit [Working 4]				26,880		26,780	53,660
less Interest on capitals	James	750		2,617		3,367	
	Peter	500				500	
	Paul	590	1,840	1,083	3,700	1,673	5,540
				25,040		23,080	48,120
less Salary (John)				—		4,000	4,000
				25,040		19,080	44,120
Residual profits	James	12,520		7,155		19,675	
	Peter	8,347		—		8,347	
	Paul	4,173		7,155		11,328	
	John	—	25,040	4,770	19,080	4,770	44,120

(iii)

Goodgame and Co.: Balance Sheet as at 31 December 1982

	£	£	£
Fixed assets			
Premises			120,000
Fixtures and fittings			17,550
Motor vehicles			12,250
			149,800
Current assets			
Stock [£8,400 − £2,000]		6,400	
Debtors		12,800	
Prepayments		4,040	
Bank		40,300	
		63,540	
less Current liabilities			
Creditors	10,540		
Accrued expenses	3,190	13,730	
Working capital			49,810
			199,610
Capital accounts James			65,425
Paul			27,075
John			10,000
			102,500
Current accounts James		24,142	
Paul		16,101	
John		3,770	
			44,013
			146,513
Loan (Peter) [£41,950 + £11,147]			53,097
			199,610

WORKING 1

	£	£
Revaluation of premises		60,000
Revaluation of fixtures and fittings*		7,850
		67,850
less Stock reduction in value		2,000
		65,850
*Revaluation amount		18,000
Net book value at 31 December 1982	9,800	
add back 6 months' depreciation	350	10,150
		7,850

£65,850 is credited to James, Peter and Paul 3:2:1.

WORKING 2

£30,000 is credited in old profit-sharing ratios.

WORKING 3

£25,000 (£30,000, as above, less £5,000 purchases by John) is debited to James and Paul in new ratios — that is, equally.

WORKING 4

	Jan/June £	July/Dec. £	Year £
Net profit as given	26,880	26,880	53,760
Additional depreciation on revaluation of fixture and fittings [6/12 × 5% × (£18,000 − £14,000)]		100	100
	26,880	26,780	53,660

WORKING 5: Interest on capitals

James 6/12 × 5% × £30,000
       6/12 × 8% × £65,425
Peter 6/12 × 5% × £20,000
Paul 6/12 × 5% × £23,600
       6/12 × 8% × £27,075

Question 2.2

X and T are in partnership, sharing profits and losses in the ratio of 2:1 after allowing T a salary of £4,000 per annum. The following balance sheet has just been completed at 31 May 1983.

	£	£		£	£
CAPITAL ACCOUNTS			FIXED ASSETS		
X 8,000			Premises	10,000	
T 4,000		12,000	Machinery	8,000	18,000
CURRENT ACCOUNTS			CURRENT ASSETS		
X 2,000			Stock	5,000	
T 1,000		3,000	Debtors	2,000	7,000
CURRENT LIABILITIES					
Creditors	8,000				
Bank overdraft	2,000	10,000			
		25,000			25,000

The profits of the partnership have been low during recent years but a new business opportunity is available from 1 December 1983 requiring an additional investment of £20,000. The anticipated annual net profits from the new investment are £14,000 and it is expected that the other profits earned by the partnership will be £8,000 per annum for the foreseeable future. All profits will be accrued evenly throughout the year.

Two alternative methods to finance the necessary investment are being considered by X and T.

A. To accept into the partnership P with effect from 1 December 1983 on the following basis.
   (1) P will pay into the partnership £25,000 cash as capital.
   (2) Interest at the rate of 10 per cent per annum is to be paid on partners' fixed capital.
   (3) The balance of profits and losses are to be shared equally between the partners.
   (4) The premises are to be revalued at £28,000 immediately prior to P's admission.
B. To borrow £20,000 from a bank at a fixed nominal rate of interest of 10 per cent over 5 years repayable in equal monthly instalments. In addition, X and T will have to employ a part-time supervisor at an annual salary of £4,000 per annum.

REQUIRED

(a) The forecast profit and loss appropriation account for the year ending 31 May 1984, assuming that P is admitted to the partnership on the terms outlined above. (*Work to the nearest pound.*)   [*13 marks*]

(b) A financial statement comparing the income to be received by X and T under the two alternatives for each of the years ending 31 May 1984 and 31 May 1985. (*Work to the nearest pound.*)   [*13 marks*]

(AEB)

Answer 2.2

(a)

P, X and T: Forecast profit and loss appropriation account for year ending 31 May 1984

			June/Nov. £		*Dec./May* £	*Year* £
Net profit			4,000		11,000	15,000
less Interest on capital	P			1,250		
	X [Working 1]			1,000		
	T [Working 1]		–	500	2,750	
			4,000		8,250	
less Salary (T)			2,000		–	
			2,000		8,250	
		£				
Residual profit	P			2,750		
	X	1,333		2,750		
	T	667	2,000	2,750	8,250	

(b)

Year ending 31 May		1984		1985	
	£	£	£	£	
Profits from existing business	8,000	8,000	8,000	8,000	
Profits from new business	7,000	7,000	14,000	14,000	
	15,000	15,000	22,000	22,000	
less Bank interest	–	1,000	–	2,000	
	15,000	14,000	22,000	20,000	
less Supervisor's pay		2,000	–	4,000	
	15,000	12,000	22,000	16,000	

1984 comparison of profit appropriation

Option		A			B	
Income	P	X	T		X	T
	£	£	£		£	£
Interest on capital	1,250	1,000	500		–	–
Salary			2,000			4,000
Residual profit	2,750	4,083	3,417		4,000	4,000
	4,000	5,083	5,917		4,000	8,000

1985 comparison of profit appropriation

Option	A			B	
Income	P	X	T	X	T
	£	£	£	£	£
Interest on capital	2,500	2,000	1,000	–	–
Salary			–		4,000
Residual profit	5,500	5,500	5,500	8,000	4,000
	8,000	7,500	6,500	8,000	8,000

WORKING 1

	X	T
	£	£
Present capital	8,000	4,000
Share of revaluation	12,000	6,000
	20,000	10,000
Interest [6/12 x 10%]	1,000	500

3 Issue of Shares and Debentures

3.1 Types of capital

A limited company may raise finance either by issuing shares or by raising loans. Debentures are simply a type of loan. Shares may be further subdivided into different types, as follows.

(i) *Preference shares* are shares which carry the right to a fixed dividend before any dividend can be paid to the ordinary shareholders. Where there are insufficient profits (including those retained from previous years) to cover the preference dividend, then none can be paid and it is lost.

(ii) *Cumulative preference shares* are similar to preference shares, but if in any one year, because of the circumstances described above, the dividend is not paid it accumulates and is carried forward until such time as there are sufficient profits to cover both current dividends on the shares and the arrears.

(iii) *Ordinary shares* carry no right to a fixed dividend and dividends are decided upon once the profit is known. There is a risk of no dividend, but at the other end of the scale there is no limit on the amount.

Finally, you should appreciate that all loans, including debentures, mean that the company incurs interest charges. Interest is an expense of the company, which must be paid whether profits are earned or not. Debenture holders of the company are its creditors. Conversely, shareholders own the company and earn a right to dividends, which are an appropriation of profit.

3.2 Authorised and issued share capital

When a company is formed, it is necessary to prepare a Memorandum of Association, which is a legal document setting out its constitution and powers. Among other things, this document states the amount of share capital with which the company proposes to be registered and which is therefore the maximum amount it will be allowed to issue. However, when the company commences, it will only issue sufficient shares to raise the cash it needs.

3.3 Issues at a premium or discount

All shares and debentures have a nominal or face value (also referred to as par value). This is the amount at which they will appear in the balance sheets if they have been fully paid for. However, shares and debentures may be issued at a premium or discount to this par value. The reasons for this are not always logical, but if a company has other shares already in existence, then any further issues must be at a price near to the market price of those existing shares. This is necessary so as not to disadvantage the existing shareholders.

The share premium account is a so-called capital reserve. That is to say, it cannot be distributed to shareholders as dividends. The uses to which it may be put, as laid down by the Companies Act 1985, are:

(i) to issue bonus shares (see Section 3.6);
(ii) to write off share and debenture issue expenses and commissions;
(iii) to write off preliminary expenses;
(iv) to write off discounts allowed on shares or debentures;
(v) under certain circumstances, to provide for any premium payable on redemption (see Chapter 6).

At this point it is helpful to consider the journal entries for a share issue at a premium or discount. We could, in a simple case,

Dr. Bank
Cr. Share capital
Cr. Share premium

or

Dr. Discount on shares

You should be aware that there are legal restrictions on issuing shares at a discount, and the amount of discount must be written off (against reserves or in the profit and loss account) immediately.

In practice, we would expand the above journal entries by use of an intermediate account called an applications and allotment account, and this is demonstrated later in this chapter.

3.4 Payment by instalments

It is common for payments to be made by instalments as follows:

(i) *Application* – the amount payable by potential investors or shareholders when they apply for the shares.
(ii) *Allotment* – the amount payable when the company decides to allot the shares to the above applicants who have been successful. Often people apply for more shares than the company is issuing and one of two things may then happen. First, a ballot may be held and application monies may be returned to the unsuccessful applicants. Second, applications may be scaled down so that applicants only receive some but not all of the shares for which they applied.
(iii) *Calls* – the final amounts payable as and when called by the directors.

You should note from the worked examples that the balance sheet figure for share capital includes only amounts called up by the company (including application and allotment monies).

The accounting treatment for an issue payable by instalments is as set out in Worked Example 3.1. You should note the following: Debit bank and credit application and allotment with monies actually received. (Reverse the entry for monies refunded.) Debit application and allotment and credit both share capital and share premium with amounts due on application and allotment. Alternatively, if there is a discount, debit share discount. With debentures the procedure is identical, except that debentures are credited and not share capital.

3.5 Rights issues

Rights issues are nothing more complicated than shares offered first of all to existing shareholders. That is to say, existing shareholders have the right to apply for the shares being issued. The accounting treatment is not affected.

3.6 Bonus issues

Bonus shares are issued when there is a build-up of reserves (e.g. undistributed profits) in the company. These profits will often not be represented by cash, since the profits have been invested in other assets to expand the business. The issue of bonus shares is recorded as follows:

Dr. Profit and loss (retained earnings)
Cr. Share capital

This decreases the amount of retained earnings and increases share capital. There is no entry on cash or bank because no cash changes hands; the bonus shares are issued free.

You should realise that the shareholder receiving the shares is no better off, since, although he owns more shares, each share will now be worth less.

3.7 Forfeit of shares

Forfeit of shares arises where shares are issued payable by instalments and a shareholder fails to pay an amount due on a call. The accounting entries are

Dr. Share capital
Cr. Forfeited shares (with the nominal value or called-up value if not fully paid)

Dr. Forfeited shares
Cr. Call, application and allotment (with amounts unpaid on the shares)

The balance on the forfeited shares account now represents the amount paid by the shareholder. If the shares are then cancelled, this balance is part of the capital reserves. Often, however, they will be reissued and the entries for that reissue are then as follows:

Dr. Forfeited shares
Cr. Share capital (amount as first entry above)

Dr. Bank
Cr. Forfeited shares (monies received)

Dr. Forfeited shares
Cr. Share premium (balance on forfeited shares account)

3.8 Worked Examples

Example 3.1

The William Co. Ltd, with an Authorised Capital of £1,000,000, have already issued 600,000 £1 shares on 1 January 1983 when they offer 200,000 £1 Ordinary Shares to the public at a price of £1.50 each. The terms of issue are 50p payable on application, 80p (including the premium) on allotment and the remainder to be called later.

Applications were received by 31 January for 300,000 shares and on 2 February allotments were made as follows:

(a) 50,000 applications were refused and the money was returned to the applicants.
(b) The remainder of the shares were issued on a pro rata basis, any money overpaid being retained towards the amount due on allotment.

All money due on allotment was received by 28 February. The call for the remaining money was made on 4 April and by 30 April all but 2,000 shares had been paid for.

You are required to:

(i) Prepare journal entries to record the issue of these shares and the call made on 4 April, and

(ii) Show how the Ordinary Share Capital appears in the Balance Sheet of the Company at 30 April 1983. [*18 marks*]

NOTE : Dates and narrations are required. (OLE)

Solution 3.1

(i)

		Dr £	Cr £
Jan. 31	Bank	150,000	
	Application and allotment		150,000
	Application monies (50p per share) received from applicants for 300,000 shares		
Feb. 2	Application and allotment	25,000	
	Bank		25,000
	Return of application monies to unsuccessful applicants		
Feb.28	Bank	135,000	
	Application and allotment		135,000
	Balance of allotment monies received in respect of 200,000 shares (due on allotment £160,000 less £25,000 overpaid with application monies)		
Feb. 2	Application and allotment	260,000	
	Ordinary share capital		160,000
	Share premium		100,000
	Application and allotment of 200,000 £1 ordinary shares, 50p payable on application and 80p (including 30p premium) payable on allotment		

		Dr. £	Cr. £
Apr. 4	First call	40,000	
	Ordinary share capital		40,000
	First call of 20p on 200,000 £1 Ordinary shares		
Apr. 30	Bank	39,600	
	First call		39,600
	Monies received on first call		

(ii)

Ordinary share capital

	£
Issued £1 Ordinary shares 800,000	800,000
Share premium	100,000

Additionally, the authorised share capital will appear by way of note.

The balance on the first call account of £400 will appear as a debtor on the balance sheet.

Example 3.2

Growfast Ltd, having established itself as a manufacturer of plastic products, is now in a position to expand its production. The company is considering three alternative ways of financing the £2,000,000 required to purchase the fixed assets. It is company policy to depreciate fixed assets at the rate of 10 per cent per annum on cost.

Alternative (1) To issue 1,000,000 £1 ordinary shares at £2 per share. The directors of the company intend to continue to pay dividends of 15 per cent per annum.

Alternative (2) To issue at a discount of 3 per cent £1,500,000 in 12 per cent debentures redeemable in ten years' time. The discount is to be written off over the ten-year period. The remaining fixed assets that are required are to be hired from Hirers Ltd over a ten-year period at an annual rental of £65,000.

Alternative (3) To purchase the fixed assets on credit. The terms of the credit agreement provide for five annual instalments of £450,000 each. Assume that interest accrues evenly over the period of the loan.

REQUIRED

(a) In respect of **each** of the above alternatives, the entries which would appear in the revenue accounts of the company at the end of the first year, showing clearly the section of the revenue account which would be affected. [8 marks]

(b) The relevant extracts from the balance sheet of Growfast Ltd at the end of the first year for **each** of the above alternatives. [7 marks]

(c) Discuss the implications for an existing ordinary shareholder of Growfast Ltd of **each** of the three proposals. [10 marks]

(AEB)

Solution 3.2

(a) (1) Dividends payable of 150,000 (15 per cent of nominal value) would appear as an appropriation of profit at the end of the profit and loss account after the net profit had been calculated.

27

(2) The discount of £4,500 ($\frac{1}{10}$ × 3% × £1,500,000) would appear as an expense under the heading 'interest payable' and similar charges (see Chapter 4).

The hire charges of £65,000 ($\frac{1}{10}$ × £65,000) would also appear as an expense under the heading 'cost of sales' (as it is production plant).

Debenture interest of £180,000 would appear as an expense in the profit and loss account.

(3) The interest charge of £50,000 (5 × £450,000 = £2,250,000; therefore interest charge to be spread over five years would be £250,000).

(b) (1) Share capital would increase by £1,000,000. Share premium would increase by £1,000,000.

(2) Creditors, amounts falling due after more than one year   £1,500,000
Deferred asset (discount not written off)   £41,000
It should be noted that current accounting practice may require that the hired assets be included in the balance sheet also. This would almost certainly be outside the scope of any 'A'-level syllabus.

(3) Fixed assets (less depreciation)   £2,000,000
(Assets should always be shown at their cash price.)

Creditors, amounts falling due within one year   £1,600,000
(This represents the repayment element only of future payments.)

(c) An existing shareholder might be reluctant to accept alternative (1), since if he does not have sufficient funds to purchase any of the additional shares, his stake in the company will become diluted. However, alternatives (2) and (3) expose the company (and therefore its shareholders) to additional risk, since additional profits have to be made to cover the interest charges incurred. Further, under alternative (2) the company will have to consider how it is going to redeem the debentures in ten years' time: where will the funds come from?

3.9 Further exercises

Question 3.1

A group of six young computer enthusiasts is considering forming a small business to market software and to repair certain types of hardware.

They have estimated that the total amount of capital that they require is £850,000, which they can raise in a variety of ways.

The projected operating profits for the first three years are:

Yr 1   £80,000;   Yr 2   £120,000;   Yr 3   £180,000.

They have managed to agree on the following three possible capital structures for the business:

	£
(a) Ordinary shares	400,000
10% Preference Shares	400,000
12% Bank loan	50,000
(b) Ordinary Shares	200,000
10% Preference Shares	400,000
8% Loan Stock	250,000
(c) Ordinary Shares	400,000
10% Preference Shares	200,000
8% Loan Stock	250,000

Two of the group, Bit and Byte, are interested solely in control and organisation of the business and are willing to invest £200,000 each: the others would prefer to make money and help in the business; between them they are willing to invest a further £200,000. The remainder of the capital will have to be raised outside the business.

You are required to:

(i) indicate to the group the advantages and disadvantages that each of the three suggestions offers to all the members,

and (ii) suggest one other possible way that they could organise their business.

Ignore Corporation Tax and other taxes. [*18*]

(OLE)

Answer 3.1

(i) Refer to the text for general advantages and disadvantages of each type of capital. Specifically, option (a) does not commit the company to as high a level of interest payments. Under options (b) and (c), interest charges will be $\frac{1}{4}$ of projected year 1 profits, which may be dangerously high. The table below shows the amount of interest and preference dividends payable to outside shareholders.

	(a) £	(b) £	(c) £
Interest bank loan/loan stock	6,000	20,000	20,000
Preference dividends to outsiders	20,000	–	–
	26,000	20,000	20,000

(ii) A possible alternative is cumulative preference shares (assuming those given are not).

Question 3.2

The Authorised Share Capital of a Limited Company is authorised by whom (or what)? Why could this capital differ from the Issued Capital? [*8 marks*]

(OLE)

Answer 3.2

Refer to the text: Memorandum of Association; issued share capital would differ, owing to directors not needing to issue all of the authorised share capital.

4 Limited Companies' Published Accounts

4.1 Profit and loss account format

This topic was introduced to you at 'O' level and now you must become familiar with the permitted statutory formats as laid down in the 1985 Companies Act, the most common of which are shown below.

		£	£
1.	Turnover		X
2.	Cost of sales		(X)
3.	Gross profit (or loss)		X
4.	Distribution costs	X	
5.	Administrative expenses	X	
			(X)
			X
6.	Other operating income		X
			X
7.	Income from shares in group companies	X	
8.	Income from shares in related companies	X	
9.	Income from other fixed asset investments	X	
10.	Other interest receivable and similar income	X	
			X
			X
11.	Amounts written off investments	X	
12.	Interest payable and similar charges	X	
			(X)
	Profit or loss on ordinary activities before taxation		X
13.	Tax on profit (or loss) on ordinary activities		(X)
14.	Profit (or loss) on ordinary activities after taxation		X
15.	Extraordinary income	X	
16.	Extraordinary charges	(X)	
17.	Extraordinary profit (or loss)	X	
18.	Tax on extraordinary profit (or loss)	(X)	

		X
		X
19. Other taxes not shown under the above items		(X)
20. Profit (or loss) for the financial year		X
Dividends paid and proposed		(X)
Transfers to (from) reserves		(X)
Retained profit (or loss) for the financial year		£X

Lines 2, 4 and 5 include the appropriate charge for depreciation of fixed assets. Any amounts included by way of hire costs for plant and machinery must be disclosed separately by way of notes. Similarly, auditor's remuneration must be disclosed by way of note.

Lines 15 and 16 items will be defined in chapter 4.

The published format ends with the net profit or loss for the year. However, the Act itself requires that both dividends and transfers to and from reserves should be shown separately.

4.2 Balance sheet

Again the 1985 Companies Act allows a choice of formats, and shown below is the one most commonly used.

	£	£	£
A CALLED-UP SHARE CAPITAL NOT PAID*			X
B FIXED ASSETS			
I Intangible assets			
1 Development costs	X		
2 Concessions, patents, licences, trade marks and similar rights and assets	X		
3 Goodwill	X		
4 Payments on account	X		
		X	
II Tangible assets			
1 Land and buildings	X		
2 Plant and machinery	X		
3 Fixtures, fittings, tools and equipment	X		
4 Payments on account and assets in course of construction	X		
		X	
III Investments			
1 Shares in group companies	X		
2 Loans to group companies	X		
3 Shares in related companies	X		
4 Loans to related companies	X		
5 Other investments other than loans	X		
6 Other loans	X		
7 Own shares	X		
		X	
			X

C CURRENT ASSETS
   I   Stocks
      1 Raw materials and consumables   X
      2 Work in progress   X
      3 Finished goods and goods for resale   X
      4 Payments on account   <u>X</u>

                                               X

   II Debtors
      1 Trade debtors   X
      2 Amounts owed by group companies   X
      3 Amounts owed by related companies   X
      4 Other debtors   X
      5 Called-up share capital not paid*   X
      6 Prepayments and accrued income*   <u>X</u>

                                             X

   III Investments
      1 Shares in group companies   X
      2 Own shares   X
      3 Other investments   <u>X</u>

                                           X

   IV Cash at bank and in hand   <u>X</u>

                                           X

D PREPAYMENTS AND ACCRUED INCOME*   <u>X</u>

                                           X

E CREDITORS: AMOUNTS FALLING DUE WITHIN
ONE YEAR
      1 Debenture loans   X
      2 Bank loans and overdrafts   X
      3 Payments received on account   X
      4 Trade creditors   X
      5 Bills of exchange payable   X
      6 Amounts owed to group companies   X
      7 Amounts owed to related companies   X
      8 Other creditors including taxation and
        social security   X
      9 Accruals and deferred income*   <u>X</u>

                                           <u>(X)</u>

F NET CURRENT ASSETS (LIABILITIES   <u>X</u>
G TOTAL ASSETS LESS CURRENT LIABILITIES   X

H CREDITORS: AMOUNTS FALLING DUE AFTER MORE THAN ONE YEAR

1 Debenture loans	X		
2 Bank loans and overdrafts	X		
3 Payments received on account	X		
4 Trade creditors	X		
5 Bills of exchange payable	X		
6 Amounts owed to group companies	X		
7 Amounts owed to related companies	X		
8 Other creditors including taxation and social security	X		
9 Accruals and deferred income*	X		
		X	

I PROVISIONS FOR LIABILITIES AND CHARGES

1 Pensions and similar obligations	X		
2 Taxation, including deferred taxation	X		
3 Other provisions	X		
		X	

J ACCRUALS AND DEFERRED INCOME*

		X	
			(X)
			X
		£	£

K CAPITAL AND RESERVES

I Called-up share capital		X
II Share premium account		X
III Revaluation reserve		X
IV Other reserves:		
1 Capital redemption reserve	X	
2 Reserve for own shares	X	
3 Reserves provided for by the articles of association	X	
4 Other reserves	X	
		X
V Profit and loss account		X
		£X

*These items may be shown in either/any one of the positions indicated.

Fixed assets may be valued at cost or a revalued amount. In the latter case the difference between cost and the revalued amount must be shown as a revaluation reserve (K. III) and not included as profit.

Additional information for fixed assets must be provided. For each category we must detail cost (or valuation) at the beginning of the year and show additions and disposals, and the effect of revaluations during the year; this should then lead to cost (or revaluation) at the end of the year. Similarly, for the depreciation provisions we must show the balance at the beginning of the year and the charge for the year, the write-back on disposals, and so arrive at the year-end balances for depreciation provisions. Worked Example 4.3 illustrates this requirement.

Called-up share capital is the amount paid and amounts due but unpaid at the balance sheet date. The accounting treatment was discussed further in Chapter 3 but here we should note that a company must make additional disclosure of (a) the authorised share capital as stated in its memorandum of association; (b) the number and aggregate value of shares of each class allotted (e.g. preference and ordinary).

In the capital and reserves section, be aware that some reserves are distributable by way of dividends (e.g. profit and loss account balance). Others (e.g. share premium and revaluation reserve) may not be distributed by way of dividend.

Finally, there is a requirement to show by way of note any contingent liabilities; these are explained in Chapter 5. Specifically we must provide details of: (a) contracts for capital expenditure not provided for; (b) capital expenditure authorised by the directors which has not been contracted for.

4.3 Worked examples

Example 4.1

The White Valley Trading plc has the following balances in its books at 31 May 1986:

	£		£
Premises at cost	3,000,000	Preference dividend paid	70,000
Furniture and Fittings at cost	726,000	Debenture interest paid	80,000
Motor Vehicles at cost	450,000	ACT owing	154,900
Equipment at cost	82,400	ACT recoverable	308,571
Stocks at 1 June 1985	65,700	Goodwill	262,000
Trade Creditors	42,000	Share Premium	83,000
Investments in Green Vale plc	54,000	Capital Reserve	56,000
Administration expenses	152,600	Bank balance (debit)	358,000
Selling and Distribution expenses	254,529	Prepayments	5,400
Purchases of goods for resale	1,720,000	Profit and Loss A/C 1 June 1985	120,400
Sales	3,430,000	Share Capital	2,200,000
Trade Debtors	152,300	Provision for depreciation:	
Returns Inwards	20,000	Furniture and Fittings	280,000
Returns Outwards	30,000	Motor Vehicles	210,000
Discounts Allowed	14,000	Equipment	22,200
Discounts Received	22,000	Other reserves	70,000
8% Debentures	1,000,000	Debenture Redemption Reserve	150,000
Patents and Trade Marks	95,000		

NOTES

1. Included in the administration expenses are:

Depreciation — Furniture and Fittings	£72,600
Equipment	£3,090

2. Included in Selling and Distribution expenses are:

Depreciation — Motor Vehicles	£45,000
Equipment	£1,030

3. Stocks at 31 May 1986   £74,100

4. Amounts owing at 31 May 1986 are:

Directors' Fees	£8,000
Auditors' Fees	£4,200

5. The Directors propose to transfer:

    £50,000 to Debenture Redemption Reserve

    £30,000 to other reserves

    and to pay a dividend to the ordinary shareholders of 15p per share.

6. The Authorised Share Capital of the company is £3,000,000; of this all the preference shares of 10% have been issued and £1,500,000 of the ordinary shares. All the shares have a nominal value of £1.

7. The Corporation tax on the year's profits is estimated to be £580,200.

8. Green Vale plc is a subsidiary of White Valley Trading.

9. £400,000 of the debentures are redeemable in January 1987.

You are required to:

(a) Calculate the Profit and Loss Account balance that would be included in the Balance Sheet at 31 May 1986,

(b) List in good order and total the items which you would include under the following headings in the published Balance Sheet:

   (i) Intangible Fixed Assets

  (ii) Tangible Fixed Assets

(iii) Current Assets

(iv) Creditors' amounts falling due within one year

 (v) Total Assets less Current Liabilities

(vi) Capital and Reserves

(c) Show what information would be shown in the fixed assets schedule attached to the accounts,

(d) Show the note concerning the called up share capital,

(e) Calculate the total of the published Balance Sheet.

Ignore ACT on Proposed Dividends   [40]

                                                             (O)

Solution 4.1

(a)

White Valley Trading plc: Profit and loss account for year ended 31 May 1986

	£	£
Sales [£3,430,000 − £20,000]		3,410,000
Cost of Sales		
Opening stock	65,700	
Purchases [£1,720,000 − £30,000]	1,690,000	
	1,755,700	
less Closing stock	74,100	(1,681,600)
Gross profit		1,728,400
Distribution costs	254,529	
Administrative expenses [Working 1]	156,800	(411,329)
		1,317,071
Interest payable		(80,000)
		1,237,071
Taxation		(580,200)
		656,871
Dividends payable [£70,000 + £225,000]		(295,000)
Profit retained		£ 361,871
Retained profit for the year		361,871
less Transfer to debenture redemption reserve	50,000	
Transfer to other reserves	30,000	(80,000)
		281,871
add Retained profit from previous years		120,400
		402,271

WORKING 1: Administrative expenses

	£
As given	152,600
Discounts allowed	14,000
Directors' fees owing	8,000
Audit fee owing	4,200
	178,800
less Discounts received	22,000
	156,800

(b)

White Valley Trading plc: Balance Sheet as at 31 May 1986

	£	£	£
Fixed assets			
Intangible assets [£262,000 + £95,000]			357,000
Tangible assets [refer to answer to part (c)]			3,746,200
Investments			54,000
			4,157,200
Current assets			
Stocks		74,100	
Debtors [£152,300 + £5,400 + £308,571]		466,271	
Bank		358,000	
		898,371	
less Creditors' amounts falling due within one year			
Debentures	400,000		
Trade creditors	42,000		
Others*	960,100		
Accruals [£8,000 + £4,200]	12,200	1,414,300	
Net Current liabilities			(515,929)
Total Assets less Current liabilities			3,641,271
Creditors: amounts falling due after more than one year			
Debentures			(600,000)
Net Assets			3,041,271
Capital and reserves			
Share capital			2,200,000
Share premium			83,000
Debenture redemption reserve			200,000
Capital reserve			56,000
Other reserves			100,000
Profit and loss account			402,271
			3,041,271

*Other creditors

	£
ACT [refer to Section 5.7 for explanation]	154,900
Corporation tax	580,200
Dividends	225,000
	960,100

While the full balance sheet is not required by the question, it is shown here for illustrative purposes.

(c)

Fixed assets:

	Cost £	Depreciation £	Net book value £
Land and buildings	3,000,000		3,000,000
Furniture and fittings*	726,000	280,000	446,000
Motor vehicles*	450,000	210,000	240,000
Equipment*	82,400	22,200	60,200
	4,258,400	512,200	3,746,200

*These may be combined and described as Fixtures, fittings, tools and equipment.

(d)

Share capital:

	Authorised £	Issued £
£1 10% Preference shares	700,000	700,000
£1 Ordinary shares	2,300,000	1,500,000
	3,000,000	2,200,000

(e) Refer to answer to part (b).

Example 4.2

The Companies Act 1981 requires the following to be shown:
Turnover; Cost of sales; Administration expenses; and Distribution expenses. When calculating the amounts to be shown under these headings, which category would each of the following fall into? Hire of plant and machinery; Directors' fees; Depreciation of shop fittings; Returns inwards

State your reason for choosing the respective category. *(8 marks)*
(OLE)

Solution 4.2

Hire of plant and machinery: Cost of sales, since it is a production cost.

Directors' fees: Administrative expenses, assuming they are paid to directors who do not have specific duties and are involved in the general administration of the company.

Depreciation of shop fittings: Distribution costs, since the shop is used as a selling function.

Returns inward: Turnover (returns inward are a deduction from the gross sales figure).

Example 4.3

At 1 January 1984 a company had the following assets:

	Cost £	Depreciation to 31.12.83 £
Premises	1,200,000	nil
Plant and Machinery	950,000	413,500
Fixtures and Fittings	218,000	37,200
Motor Vehicles	410,000	242,620

37

The company depreciates its assets at the following rates per annum, a full year's depreciation being provided in the year of purchase, but none in the year of sale.

Plant and Machinery	10%	(Straight Line/Fixed Instalment)
Fixtures and Fittings	5%	(Straight Line/Fixed Instalment)
Motor Vehicles	20%	(Diminishing Balance/Reducing Instalment)

During the year ending 31 December 1984 the following transactions took place:
1. The Directors decided to revalue the premises to £1,500,000.
2. Plant and Machinery purchased in 1980 for £200,000 was sold in October 1984 for £130,000.
3. A Motor Van purchased in July 1982 for £42,000 was sold in December 1984 for £24,000.
4. During the year the following assets were purchased:

Plant and Machinery	£150,000
Fixtures and Fittings	£10,000
Motor Vehicles	£62,000

5. Plant and Machinery which cost £40,000 is at least eleven years old at 31 December 1984.

You are required to prepare a Schedule of Fixed Assets for inclusion in the accounts to be published for the year ending 31 December 1984, and to show the profit or loss on sale of fixed assets during the year.　　　　　　　　　　　　　　　　　　　*[18]*

(OLE)

Solution 4.3

Fixed Assets
1. Cost

	Premises	Plant and machinery	Fixtures and fittings	Motor vehicles
	£	£	£	£
At 1 January 1984	1,200,000	950,000	218,000	410,000
Revaluation	300,000			
Purchases		150,000	10,000	62,000
Disposals		(200,000)		(42,000)
At 31 December 1984	1,500,000	900,000	228,000	430,000

2. Depreciation

At 1 January 1984	–	413,500	37,200	242,620
Charge for year	–	86,000*	11,400†	40,500 [Working 1]
Disposals	–	(80,000)	–	(15,120)
At 31 December 1984	–	419,500	48,600	268,000

*10% × (£900,000 − £40,000)
† 5% × £228,000

WORKING 1	£
Opening Net book value	167,380
less Net book value of disposal (£42,000 − £15,120)	26,880
	140,500
add Purchase	62,000
Net book value to be depreciated by 20%	202,500

Calculation of profit/(loss) on sale	Plant and machinery	Motor vehicles
	£	£
Cost	200,000	42,000
Depreciation to date	80,000	15,120
Net book value	120,000	26,880
Proceeds	130,000	24,000
Profit/(loss) on disposal	10,000	(2,880)

4.4 Further exercises

Question 4.1

Stonewall Company Limited commenced business on 1 May 1982 with an authorised capital of 500,000 £1 ordinary shares. The following information, extracted from the accounts after a manufacturing account has been prepared, relates to the first year ended 30 April 1983.

	£	£
£1 Ordinary shares issued and fully paid		200,000
10% Debentures (issued 1 November 1982)		50,000
Share premium		25,000
Trade debtors and creditors	18,000	10,000
Plant and machinery at cost	100,000	
Bank	40,000	
Property at cost	60,000	
Motor vehicles	30,000	
Sales		700,000
Factory cost of manufactured goods	400,000	
Establishment expenses	130,000	
Interim ordinary dividend	12,000	
Selling and distribution expenses	50,000	
Administration expenses	160,000	
Stock of raw materials	20,000	
Factory overhead accrued		15,000
Provision for depreciation of plant and machinery		20,000
	1,020,000	1,020,000

The following additional information is given.
(1) Establishment expenses include directors' emoluments of £60,000.
(2) It is proposed to declare a final ordinary share dividend which would make the total dividend for the year 10 per cent.
(3) The closing stock of finished goods is valued at £75,000.
(4) Motor vehicles are to be depreciated at 25 per cent on cost. Such depreciation is to be included as part of selling and distribution expenses.
(5) The property is to be shown in the accounts at 30 April 1983 at £100,000, following a survey by a chartered surveyor quoting that to be the current market value.

REQUIRED

(a) The trading and profit and loss account for the year ended 30 April 1983 of Stonewall Company Limited. [8 marks]
(b) The balance sheet as at 30 April 1983 of Stonewall Company Limited. [12 marks]

(c) To what extent must the following items in the accounts of Stonewall Company Limited be disclosed to satisfy the requirements of the Companies Act?
 (i) Establishment expenses
 (ii) Selling and distribution expenses
 (iii) Proposed dividends
 (iv) Gross profit

[*3 marks*]

(AEB)

Solution 4.1

(a)

Stonewall Company Limited: Profit and Loss Account for year ended 30 April 1983

	£	£
Turnover		700,000
Cost of sales		
Factory cost of manufactured goods	400,000	
Closing stock of finished goods	(75,000)	325,000
Gross profit		375,000
Distribution costs [£50,000 + £7,500]	57,500	
Administrative expenses [£160,000 + £130,000]	290,000	(347,500)
		27,500
Interest payable		2,500
Net profit		25,000
Dividends		20,000
Retained profit		5,000

(b)

Stonewall Company Limited: Balance Sheet as at 30 April 1983

	£	£	£
Fixed assets			
Land and buildings			100,000
Plant and machinery [£100,000 − £20,000]			80,000
Motor vehicles [£30,000 − £7,500]			22,500
			202,500
Current assets			
Stock [£20,000 + £75,000]		95,000	
Debtors		18,000	
Bank		40,000	
		153,000	
less Creditors amounts falling due within one year			
Trade creditors	10,000		
Other [Working 1]	25,500	35,500	
Net Current assets			117,500
Total Assets less Current liabilities			320,000
less Creditors amounts falling due after more than one year			
Debentures			50,000
Net Assets			£270,000
Capital and reserves			
£1 Ordinary Shares [authorised 500,000]			200,000
Share premium			25,000
Revaluation reserve			40,000
Profit and loss account			5,000
			270,000

WORKING 1: Other creditors

	£
Dividend	8,000
Interest	2,500
Factory overhead accrued	15,000
	25,500

(c) (i) May be included with administrative expenses.
     (ii) and (iv) refer to text; must all be disclosed separately.
     (iii) To be included with dividends paid and proposed.

Question 4.2

Define 'Contingent liability'. Give two examples of such liabilities and explain where they would be shown in the published accounts of a company.   [*8 marks*]

(OLE)

Answer 4.2

Refer to the text.

Question 4.3

The following draft balance sheet of Hunt Ltd as at 31 October 1986 has just been prepared following the completion of the revenue accounts.

FIXED ASSETS	Cost	Aggregate Depreciation	
	£	£	£
FIXED ASSETS			
Plant and machinery	50,000	11,000	39,000
Fixtures	20,000	7,000	13,000
Motor vehicles	18,000	9,000	9,000
			61,000
CURRENT ASSETS			
Stock raw materials	10,000		
work in progress	4,000		
finished goods	18,000	32,000	
Debtors		11,000	
Prepayments		3,000	
Cash		4,000	
		50,000	
less CURRENT LIABILITIES			
Creditors	24,000		
Accruals	5,000		
Provisions	8,000	37,000	13,000
			74,000
CAPITAL			
Called up share capital			
40,000 £1 ordinary shares fully paid			40,000
Share premium			20,000
Profit and loss account			14,000
			74,000

41

After the preparation of the draft balance sheet the following information became available.

(1) No entry had been made in the books of the company to record the sale of a motor vehicle to a retiring member of staff. Although the sale was completed during October 1986, it has been agreed that the former employee need not pay for the vehicle until January 1987. The vehicle, which was purchased in December 1985 for £7,000, was sold to the former employee for £1,000. It is company policy to depreciate motor vehicles at the rate of 25 per cent each year based on the cost of assets shown in the accounts at the end of the financial year.

(2) Included in the closing stock of raw materials were certain items valued at cost of £5,000 which in fact can only be used to replace a cheaper component the market price of which is £3,000. In addition, the stock of finished goods has been valued at cost, although the items would cost £24,000 to purchase from another supplier.

(3) A dishonest employee has entered false purchases of £6,000 and withdrawn for his own use that amount of cash from the company's bank. In addition, in conjunction with the employee of a credit customer, returns inwards to the value of £3,000 have been entered in the books, although no goods have been returned. No money is likely to be recovered from the employee but it has been agreed with the customer that the loss on the fictitious return of goods will be borne by the customer.

(4) A provision for £8,000 had been entered in the accounts during the year ended 31 October 1985 in anticipation of legal action against the company. In fact the action had now been withdrawn.

(5) Included in the sales figure for the year ended 31 October 1986 was a payment of £750 from a customer for goods to be invoiced and delivered in December 1986.

REQUIRED

(a) A redrafted balance sheet as at 31 October 1986 of Hunt Ltd after the items above had been taken into consideration. [15 marks]

(b) Identify and discuss two relevant accounting concepts involved in the valuation of stock outlined in (2) above. [8 marks]

(AEB)

Answer 4.3

(a) Adjustments are required as follows:

	Dr £	Cr £
(1) Motor vehicle (cost)		7,000
Motor vehicle (depreciation)	1,750	
Profit and loss	4,250	
Debtors	1,000	
(2) Stock		2,000
Profit and loss	2,000	
(assuming that market price is realisable value)		
(No action regarding finished goods – see answer to part (b).)		
(3) No action, since £6,000 has already been written off for fictitious purchases. In relation to £3,000 to be recovered:		
Debtor	3,000	
Profit and loss		3,000
(4) Provisions	8,000	
Profit and loss		8,000
(5) Profit and loss	750	
Creditor (advance payments received)		750

Balance sheet figures which change are, therefore: Motor vehicles £3,750; Stocks £30,000; Debtors £15,000; Creditors (advance payments) £750; Provisions £nil; Profit and loss £18,000.

(b) Prudence concept: value at lower of cost and net realisable value. Matching concept: do not recognise profit on sale of finished goods until goods have been sold.

5 Statements of Standard Accounting Practice

5.1 Introduction

Prior to 1981 the Companies Acts were generally deficient in the regulation of accounting principles, and even with what has now become the 1985 Companies Act there are still many different bases which can be used legally in the preparation of accounts. The bases of stock valuation and calculation of the depreciation charge are two examples.

This weakness has been overcome to an important degree by the issuing of Statements of Standard Accounting Practice (SSAPs) by the major accountancy bodies. The object of these SSAPs is first and foremost to ensure a degree of standardisation and uniformity in the preparation of accounts. Where, for various reasons, this uniformity cannot be achieved, the SSAPs require that companies must make sufficient disclosure (of, for example, bases and policies) to give users of accounting information a fuller picture of the facts as they would wish to know them.

Since the first was issued in the early 1970s further SSAPs have been issued and existing ones revised or withdrawn. Below are listed the SSAPs relevant to the 'A' level syllabus.

5.2 SSAP2: Disclosure of accounting policies

Chapter 1 dealt with the fundamental accounting concepts covered by the SSAP. In applying these concepts companies may still use different bases of accounting (e.g. stock valuation). The SSAP requires that accounting policies (i.e. selection of bases) should be stated by way of a note to the accounts.

5.3 SSAP3: Earnings per share

'Earnings' is another word for 'profit', and earnings per share is therefore the figure arrived at by taking the company's profit after tax and dividing by the number of ordinary shares issued. Thus, it can be used by investors to compare the results of a company over a period of time. For this reason SSAP3 requires that we use the profit figure after tax but before extraordinary items (defined in Section 5.6). This ensures that any trend figure is not distorted by these items.

The earnings per share figure can also be defined as the amount of profit attributable to one share in the company.

SSAP3 requires that the figure be stated on the face of the profit and loss account.

5.4 SSAP4: The accounting of treatment of Government grants

SSAP4 divides grants into revenue grants and capital grants.

Revenue grants are credited to revenue in the same period as that in which the revenue expenditure to which they relate is charged.

Capital grants are grants to cover a proportion of the costs of items of capital expenditure. These must be credited to revenue over the expected useful life of the asset, and this can be done in one of two ways:

(i) by reducing the cost of the asset by the amount of the grant and depreciating the reduced cost;

(ii) by treating the grant as a deferred credit and transferring part of it annually to the profit and loss account.

5.5 SSAP5: Accounting for value added tax

VAT (value added tax) will in most cases be added by the business to its selling price. At the same time, it will incur VAT when it purchases goods and services from its suppliers. The business will then on a quarterly basis pay over to HM Customs and Excise the amount of VAT charged on its sales less VAT incurred on its purchases.

In the circumstances outlined above, both sales and purchases will be recorded excluding VAT. VAT charged to customers will be credited to the VAT account and VAT incurred will be debited to the VAT account. The balance on the VAT account will therefore represent the amount due to or from HM Customs and Excise, and as such should be shown as a debtor or creditor in the balance sheet.

There are circumstances in which VAT on purchases cannot be recovered. Briefly, these concern:

(i) persons not registered for VAT;

(ii) persons carrying on exempted activities (e.g. banking and insurance);

(iii) non-deductible inputs, including tax on private motor-cars and entertaining UK customers.

In any of the circumstances (i)–(iii) the VAT element must be included in the cost of the item purchased and the tax inclusive amount debited to the appropriate asset or expense account. If this procedure is followed, except in circumstances (i)–(iii) outlined above, all figures for sales, purchases and expenses will therefore be net of VAT.

5.6 SSAP6: Extraordinary items and prior year adjustments

In the Companies Act format for the published profit and loss account (Section 4.1) we referred to the separate lines for extraordinary items. SSAP6 defines these as items which derive from events or transactions outside the ordinary activities of the business and which are both material and not expected to recur frequently or regularly.

This SSAP has been and is still the subject of much debate. However, examples would be:

(i) redundancy costs related to a discontinued business;

(ii) the sale of an investment not acquired with a view to resale;

(iii) writing off intangibles due to unusual events.

The logic behind this SSAP is to give users of accounts an indication of the trend in profits and level of profitability undistorted by those extraordinary items.

5.7 SSAP8: Treatment of taxation under the imputation system

The only knowledge required of SSAP8 is that the tax charge will appear as a charge in the profit and loss account on the appropriate line. You should notice that dividends are paid out of profits which have themselves already been subject to tax by way of corporation tax. For this reason dividends are deemed to be paid net of tax and no further tax is usually payable by the recipient.

In calculating the taxation charge in the profit and loss account, an estimate will usually be required to be made, since the exact liability will not have been finalised. Any over- or under-provision, when the taxation charge is finalised, will be adjusted in the following year's profit and loss account in the same way as any other over- or under-accrual.

The taxation charge will usually be paid sometime after the company's year end. However, when a dividend is paid, a company is required to make an advance payment of corporation tax or ACT (advance corporation tax). The amount of this ACT is then deducted from the total corporation tax liability when that latter liability becomes due.

5.8 SSAP9: Stocks and work in progress

Chapter 14 covers the points you need to know about SSAP9.

5.9 SSAP10: Statements of source and application of funds

Chapter 19 fully discusses this topic.

5.10 SSAP12: Accounting for depreciation

SSAP12 requires that all fixed assets having a finite useful life be depreciated. The major item of fixed assets not requiring to be depreciated will therefore be free-hold land.

SSAP12 recommends no particular method, but requires businesses to allocate depreciation as fairly as possible to periods expected to benefit from the use of the asset. Thus, any one of straight line, reducing balancing, sum of digits, depletion unit, machine hour or revaluation methods might be appropriate.

5.11 SSAP13: Accounting for research and development

SSAP13 deals with the occasions when development costs may be deferred to future periods by treating them as an asset in the balance sheet under intangible assets.

Research costs, whether pure or applied, should always be regarded as a continuing operation and therefore written off as they are incurred.

Development costs may be deferred when:

   (i) there is a clearly defined development project, and the related expenditure on this project is separately identifiable;

  (ii) the expected outcome of the project has been assessed, and there is reasonable certainty that

      (a) it is technically feasible, and

      (b) it is commercially viable;

 (iii) the eventual profits from the developed product or system will be sufficient to cover past and future costs;

 (iv) the company has adequate resources to complete the development project.

If any of these conditions is not satisfied, the development costs should be written off in the year of the expenditure.

5.12 SSAP14: Group accounts

The topic of SSAP14 is mostly outside the scope of 'A' level syllabuses. However, an elementary knowledge is necessary.

Where a company owns more than 50 per cent of another company, that company is a subsidiary of the first company. SSAP14 requires companies with subsidiaries to prepare group accounts including a consolidated profit and loss account and balance sheet. These consolidated or group accounts will incorporate the figures (assets, liabilities, revenues and expenses) for the holding company itself and its subsidiary company or companies.

Where the subsidiary is not fully owned, the total profit of that subsidiary is incorporated in the group accounts initially, with a deduction shown for that share of the subsidiary company's profits attributable to outside (or minority) shareholders. Similarly, all of the subsidiary company's assets are included in the group balance sheet and that proportion owned by outside shareholders is shown elsewhere as minority interest.

5.13 SSAP17: Accounting for post-balance sheet events

SSAP17 requires that any information coming to light after the balance sheet date, but before the accounts have been signed by the directors, should not be ignored. If that information alters our opinion as to the value of an asset or the amount of a liability at the balance sheet date, then we should adjust the accounts accordingly. Any information which does not so alter our opinion, but which would be of interest to users of accounts, should be disclosed by way of note.

5.14 SSAP18: Accounting for contingencies

A contingency is a condition which exists at the balance sheet date where the outcome will be confirmed only on the occurrence or non-occurrence of one or more uncertain future events. A contingent gain or loss is a gain or loss dependent on a contingency.

We noted in Chapter 4 that, where contingencies have not been provided for in the accounts, further information must be given by way of note.

SSAP18 recommends the following treatments dependent upon likelihood.

(i) *Contingent losses* If it is probable that a loss will result, then provide for it. If it is reasonably possible that a loss will result, then disclose it by way of note only. Otherwise ignore.

(ii) *Contingent gains* If a gain is probable, then disclose it by way of note. If a gain is less than probable, then ignore it. Contingent gain must be a near-certainty before an 'accrual' in the profit for the year becomes appropriate.

5.15 SSAP22: Accounting for goodwill

The appropriate parts of SSAP22 are discussed in Chapter 7.

5.16 Worked examples

Example 5.1

Systemic Microcomputers p.l.c. are manufacturers of products which require a significant amount of 'research and development' expenditure. At the end of the company's financial year on 31 May 1986, an analysis of the general ledger account for 'research and development' expenditure showed the following:

	£
Cost of scientific apparatus	20,000
Cost of installing scientific apparatus	18,960
Salaries paid to staff engaged in pure research	31,200
Salaries paid to staff engaged on the development of a new product, codenamed 'Tudor'	43,750
Salaries paid to staff engaged on the development of a new product, codenamed 'York'	28,120
	142,030
Less government grant received towards cost of scientific apparatus	4,000
	138,030

Notes

1. 'Tudor' is expected to become a viable and profitable addition to the existing product range.
2. 'York' has now been abandoned due to pressure from rival manufacturers.
3. A competitor, Macro Limited, is claiming £50,000 damages from the company for the alleged infringement of a patent which Macro Limited owns.
4. At a meeting held in April 1986, the company's directors authorised the purchase of laboratory equipment valued at £72,000. By 31 May 1986, contracts had been signed for two-thirds of this equipment.

Note: the company depreciates all tangible fixed assets over five years, with a full year's depreciation being charged in the year of purchase.

(a) Calculate the amounts to be included in the published profit and loss account and/or published balance sheet for each of the six items listed in the above analysis. Give reasons for the particular treatment adopted. [*17 marks*]

(b) The managing director of Systemic Microcomputers p.l.c. has asked for advice as to whether any reference to the matters contained in notes 3 and 4 above should be made in the financial statements for the year to 31 May 1986. Advise the managing director. [*8 marks*]

(L)

Solution 5.1

(a) (i)
Balance sheet extracts

	£
Tangible fixed assets	
Equipment at cost (including installation)	38,960
less grant	4,000
	34,960
Depreciation charged to profit and loss	6,992*
Net book value	27,968

* Alternatively

Depreciation $\frac{1}{5} \times £38,960 =$	7,792
and Grant credited to profit and loss	800

Intangible fixed assets	
Development costs (Tudor project)	43,750

(ii)
Profit and loss extracts

Salaries paid to research staff	31,200
Salaries paid to staff re York project	28,120
Depreciation as above	6,992

(b) Claim for damages should be referred to by way of note as contingent liability.
   Capital expenditure agreed to but not contracted for is specifically required by the 1985 Companies Act to appear by way of note as contingent liability (refer to Section 4.2).
   'Contracted for' must be shown separately from 'authorised but not yet contracted for'.

Example 5.2

The managing director of a limited company has been told by the company's auditors that published financial statements should comply not only with relevant Acts of Parliament, but also with statements of standard accounting practice (SSAPs).

(a) Examples of areas covered by SSAPs include: (1) depreciation, (2) research and development expenditure and (3) stocks and work in progress. Explain the reasons for standardising the accounting procedures in relation to one of these areas.   [*8 marks*]
(b) Explain the significance of SSAPs to the accounting profession and the users of accounting information.   [*12 marks*]
(L)

Solution 5.2

(a) Refer to the text. The key point is that standardisation ensures that in a given set of circumstances accounts of different companies should use similar bases.
(b) The accounting profession is obliged to follow SSAPs in the preparation of accounts. When acting as auditors, accountants are required to draw the shareholders' attention to any occasions where an SSAP has not been complied with. The user of accounts can use the information, knowing that the accounts have been prepared in accordance with sound principles and are not unduly

influenced by subjective opinions. On the seamier side, it also gives less room to directors and others who may wish to manipulate accounting information for some reason.

Example 5.3

The Companies Act 1985 uses the terms 'Extraordinary charges' and 'Extraordinary profit or loss' in the format for Profit and Loss Accounts. What do you understand these terms to mean?

(OLE)

Solution 5.3

Refer to the text.

5.17 Further exercises

Question 5.1

What is VAT, who pays it and who receives it? Explain with a simple example how VAT would be accounted for in the books of a retailer, and state where the balance of the account would appear in the final accounts.

[8]

(OLE)

Answer 5.1

A tax payable on sales and services. A business charges VAT to its customers. A business pays to HM Customs and Excise tax charged to tax customers less tax it has suffered on its own purchases. Sales and purchases are accounted for net; VAT is posted to a VAT account, which is then equivalent to a personal account of HM Customs and Excise. The balance on the VAT account would appear as debtor or creditor in the balance sheet.

Question 5.2

What is meant by an 'SSAP'? How are they of use to accountants? Name two accounting subjects that are covered by SSAPs.

[8]

(OLE)

Answer 5.2

Refer to the text.

Question 5.3

(i) The consolidated balance sheet of a large public limited company included the following descriptions:

(a) Intangible assets
(b) Creditors: amounts falling due after more than one year
(c) Minority shareholders' interest

(d) Called-up share capital

(e) Reserves

Explain briefly the meaning of each of the five terms. [*10 marks*]

(ii) The annual report of the company included a figure of 39.4p for 'earnings per share'. This was calculated by dividing the profit before extraordinary items by the number of ordinary shares in issue at the balance sheet date.

Why is the 'earnings per share' figure given, and why are 'extraordinary items' excluded from the calculations? [*5 marks*]

(L)

Answer 5.3

(i) Refer to the text for further detail, but key points are:

    (a) Fixed assets which are not physical assets.

    (b) Liabilities of the company payable within one year.

    (c) Interest of outside shareholders in assets of subsidiary company or companies.

    (d) Share capital issued and payable (refer to Section 3.4).

    (e) Undistributed profits.

(ii) To give shareholders an indication of the performance of the company — for example, to compare with previous years. Particularly useful where straight comparison of profit figures would be distorted by fluctuating number of shares in issue. Extraordinary items are excluded, as they would distort trend.

6 Redemption of Shares and Debentures

6.1 Redemption of debentures

In the straightforward case of repaying debentures the entry will be

Cr. Bank
Dr. Debentures

This will eliminate the liability and is all that needs to be done. However, because of the strain on the bank balance, many companies set aside out of profits annually an amount to provide for the redemption; this is done as follows:

Dr. Profit and loss
Cr. Debenture redemption reserve

The debenture redemption reserve is part of the total reserves of the company making up the shareholders' funds. By doing this the company is indicating that it is not intending to distribute those reserves by way of dividends.

6.2 Redemption of shares

The 1985 Companies Act gives a company power to issue both redeemable preference shares and redeemable ordinary shares. While giving this power, the Act also ensures that creditors (including debenture holders) are protected. This is necessary, since on a winding up of the company the shareholders rank last in order of payment and, if it were not for the above protection, a troubled company could use share redemption to give preferential treatment to its shareholders.

The protection is given by requiring that shares can only be redeemed from one or both of the following:

(i) the proceeds of a new issue;
(ii) out of profits, which involves transferring an amount equivalent to the cost of redemption from distributable reserves to non-distributable reserves.

This will ensure that the balance sheet figure for share capital and non-distributable reserves is not reduced. An understanding of this basic objective will help you to understand the journal entries involved, particularly when share premiums make the situation a little more complex.

Referring back to (i) and (ii) above, you will appreciate that, in the case of a new issue of shares to finance redemption of others, the only change on the balance sheet is a substitution of old shares by new shares. Where the redemption is financed by method (ii), the journal entry is as follows:

Dr. Profit and loss
Cr. Capital redemption reserve

This is similar to the journal entry described in Section 6.1, which the company made voluntarily, whereas in the case of share redemption there is a legal requirement for it.

We shall now consider the case of redeeming shares at a premium. This will normally be done as follows:

Dr. Share capital (nominal value of shares redeemed)
Dr. Profit and loss (premium payable on redemption)
Cr. Bank (cost of redemption)

The above reflects the final effect on the balance sheet; however, theoretically a share redemption account should be used as follows:

Dr. Share capital
Cr. Share redemption

followed by

Dr. Share redemption
Cr. Bank

However, where the shares were originally issued at premium, the company may debit share premium account with the premium on redemption, provided that:

(i) the redemption is financed by a fresh issue of shares;
(ii) the premium does not exceed the lower of
   (a) the premium received on the issue of the shares redeemed,
   (b) the current balance on the share premium account (including premiums on the new issue).

Where redemption is financed only partly by the issue of new shares at premium, we must consider how much needs to be transferred to the capital redemption reserve. The more generally accepted view of the legal requirement is as follows: transfer to capital redemption reserve the nominal value of the shares redeemed less the proceeds (including premium) of the new issue.

6.3 Purchase of company's own shares

Subject to observing the legal requirements, companies may purchase their own shares. The accounting treatment is then almost identical with that for share redemption. Public companies must either finance the purchase by a new issue of shares or by capitalising distributable profits. Private companies are not so restricted but they have to meet further legal requirements.

A company will use this method where there is no power of redemption contained in the company's articles of association.

6.4 Worked examples

Example 6.1

A company has an authorised capital of 2,000,000 £1 shares, of which 1,500,000 have been issued. At 31 May 1985 the balance sheet of the company shows the following items:

	£
Premium account	82,000
Profit and loss account	515,000
£1 Ordinary shares	1,000,000
8% Preference shares (issued at a premium)	500,000
6% Convertible stock	200,000

The following transactions took place during the year ending 31 May 1986:

June 1985 A rights issue was made of 200,000 Ordinary shares at £1.50 each. These rights were all taken up and the proceeds received by the end of the month.

July 1985 The 8 per cent redeemable preference shares were redeemed at a premium of 5 per cent.

July 1985 Half of the stockholders opted to convert their stock to Ordinary shares at a rate of three shares for each £4 of stock held.

Aug 1985 The company made a bonus issue of one ordinary share for every five shares held at that date.

You are required to show:
The journal entries, with narrations, to record the above transactions.

[*18 marks*]
(OLE)

Solution 6.1

	Dr. £	Cr. £
Bank	300,000	
Ordinary share capital		200,000
Share premium		100,000

Issue of 200,000 £1 Ordinary shares at £1 each

	£	£
8% Preference share capital	500,000	
Share premium	25,000	
Bank		525,000

Redemption of 8% Preference shares at premium of 5%

6% convertible stock	100,000	
Ordinary share capital		75,000
Share premium		25,000

Conversion of loan stock to ordinary shares on basis of 3 for 4

Profit and loss account	255,000	
Ordinary share capital		255,000*

Issue of bonus shares on basis of 1 for 5

* $\frac{1}{5} \times$ (£1,000,000 + £200,000 + £75,000)

Example 6.2

Suggest reasons why a Company might issue Loan or Debenture stock at a discount and why it might redeem stock at a premium.

Solution 6.2

Refer to the text. To encourage potential investors to purchase stock. To enable a lower rate of interest to be paid because of these attractions.

Example 6.3

A company issues £60,000 Debentures at a discount of 5 per cent. The debentures are redeemable at par over six years at the rate of £10,000 per annum. If the discount is to be written off each year in proportion to the debt outstanding, calculate the charge to profit each year.

Solution 6.3

Amount outstanding at year end	*Discount to be written off*
£	£
1:60,000	$\frac{60,000}{210,000} \times 3,000 = 857$
2:50,000	$\frac{50,000}{210,000} \times 3,000 = 714$
3:40,000	$\frac{40,000}{210,000} \times 3,000 = 571$
4:30,000	$\frac{30,000}{210,000} \times 3,000 = 429$
5:20,000	$\frac{20,000}{210,000} \times 3,000 = 286$
6:10,000	$\frac{10,000}{210,000} \times 3,000 = \underline{143}$
210,000	3,000

6.5 Further exercises

Question 6.1

The following balances are in the books of the Adac plc at 20 May 1984.

	£
Ordinary Share Capital 50p per share	120,000
Preference Share Capital £1 per share	100,000
Premium on Ordinary shares	10,000
Other Reserves	18,000
Profit and Loss Account	12,000
Bank	25,000

On 1 May 1984 half of the Preference Share Capital was due to be redeemed at a premium of 5 per cent. It was decided to make a bonus issue of one ordinary share for every ten held, and to help to finance the redemption a new issue of 40,000 Ordinary shares of 50p per share was made at a price of 75p per share.

Show by journal entries how the above entries would be dealt with in the books of the company. *[18 marks]*

(OLE)

Answer 6.1

	Dr. £	Cr. £
Preference share capital	50,000	
Profit and loss account [Note 1]	2,500	
Bank		52,500

Redemption of Preference share capital at premium of 5%

Share premium [Note 2]	10,000	
Other reserves	2,000	
Ordinary share capital		12,000

Issue of bonus shares on 1 for 10 basis

Bank	30,000	
Ordinary share capital		20,000
Share premium		10,000

Issue of 40,000 50p Ordinary shares at premium of 25p

Other reserves	16,000	
Profit and loss	4,000	
Capital redemption reserve		20,000

Transfer from distributable reserves to provide for redemption of preference shares not financed by new issue (£50,000 − £30,000) [Note 3]

NOTES

(1) Refer to Section 6.2. The share premium must be charged to profit and loss, since shares were not originally issued at a premium.
(2) Refer to Section 3.3. It would be logical to utilise the share premium account balance for the bonus issue.
(3) Nominal value of shares redeemed is £50,000 less proceeds of new issue £30,000. Some accountants have suggested that in the above case we could reduce the amount needed to be transferred by a further £2,000, this £2,000 being the amount of non-distributable reserves capitalised when the bonus shares are issued. However, a strict interpretation of the 1985 Companies Act would require that £20,000 as above be transferred to the capital redemption reserve. In view of this, it would be a good idea to qualify your answer accordingly.

Question 6.2

(a) Explain why the capital and profits of a business are liabilities and not assets.
(b) A company can 'purchase' or redeem its own shares; what is the difference between these two terms? *[8 marks]*

(OLE)

Answer 6.2

(a) Both capital and profits represent the owners' investment in the company — capital by way of cash introduced and profits by way of amounts left in the business. Both amounts can therefore be deemed to be amounts due to the owners of the business by the business itself.

(b) Refer to the text. Shares may be issued as redeemable and redeemed in accordance with the terms of issue and legal requirements. A company may purchase its own ordinary shares provided that the legal requirements are fulfilled.

7 Takeovers and Mergers

7.1 Types of amalgamation

Businesses amalgamate in order that together they may achieve more than the sum total of what they would achieve by remaining independent. The amalgamation may come about as a result of:

(i) a partnership being taken over by another sole trader, a partnership or a limited company;

(ii) a partnership being taken over by another partnership or a limited company;

(iii) a limited company being taken over by another limited company;

(iv) a new company being formed to take over one or more existing businesses.

In any type of examination question on this subject you will have to deal with either the books of the new business, the books of the old business or possibly both. However, the accounting treatment will be affected little by which of the above types of amalgamation you are faced with.

7.2 Books of the old business

The steps necessary to close off the books of the old business are as follows.

(i) Transfer all assets and liability accounts which are being taken over to a realisation account, as follows:

Dr. Realisation
Cr. Various assets } assets taken over

and

Dr. Creditors
Cr. Realisation } liabilities taken over

Be sure to leave out any assets or liabilities not taken over — for example, cash and/or creditors.

(ii) If any assets are to be taken over by somebody other than the new business, then deal with these by

Dr. Cash or Purchaser or Partner's capital
Cr. Realisation (with the agreed value of these assets)

(iii) Calculate the total value of the consideration (shares, debentures and cash) being paid by the new business and deal with this by

Dr. Purchaser of business
Cr. Realisation

(iv) In the case of a company being taken over, transfer to a sundry members account the balances on ordinary share capital, reserves and intangible or fictitious assets as follows:

    Dr.   Ordinary share capital
    Dr.   Reserves (e.g. profit and loss, share premium, etc.)
    Cr.   Goodwill
    Cr.   Sundry members

(v) Ascertain the balance on the realisation account. This will represent a profit or loss on realisation and should be transferred to capital account(s) (in the case of sole traders and partnerships) or sundry members account (in the case of a company). In other words,

    Dr./Cr.   Realisation
    Dr./Cr.   Capital or Sundry members (with balance on realisation account)

(vi) Deal with the consideration being received from the new business as follows:

    Dr.   Cash (with cash part of consideration)
    Dr.   Sundry members (with value of shares in new business issued to them)*
    Dr.   Debentures or preference shares (with any part of the consideration received by them)*
    Cr.   Purchaser of business (with total purchase consideration)

Note that you may also find that the debit at first is to an account called 'shares in new company' account. If this is so, this account will then be credited at a later time with a debit to the accounts asterisked above.

(vii) Pay any liabilities which the old business itself has to settle by

    Dr.   Creditors
    Cr.   Bank

(viii) Any balance on the bank account should now be equal to an opposite balance on capital (sole traders or partnerships) or sundry members (company). This balance will be used to settle the liability to them as follows:

    Dr.   Capital or Sundry members
    Cr.   Bank

All of the accounts in the books of the old business should now be closed.

7.3 Books of the new business

It is important to ascertain the values at which the assets, in particular, are to be recorded in the books of the new business. The entries will then be as follows:

(i) Dr.   Various assets (with agreed values)
    Cr.   Liabilities (with liabilities taken over)
    Cr.   Purchase of business (with total consideration paid for those assets and liabilities)
    Dr.   Goodwill (balancing figure)*

The item asterisked is the difference between the price paid for the business as a whole and the total values of the individual assets less liabilities. If the figure is negative there will be a credit to capital reserve.

(ii) Dr. Purchase of business (total consideration as above)
     Cr. Cash (with cash part of consideration)
     Cr. Share capital (nominal value of shares issued as consideration)
     Cr. Share premium (agreed value less nominal value of shares issued as consideration)

In simple cases you may find that the purchase of business account is by-passed and journal entries (i) and (ii) above are then combined with the purchase of business account omitted.

7.4 Worked examples

Example 7.1

On 30 April 1986 a new company, Rainbow plc, was formed to take over three existing companies. The authorised capital of Rainbow plc was to consist of 1,000,000 Ordinary Share of 50p each.

The terms of the takeover were as follows:

BLUE plc   The creditors and all the assets with the exception of the bank to be taken over at book values, settlement to be: nine ordinary shares in Rainbow for every fifty ordinary shares in Blue. Four ordinary shares in Rainbow for every two preference shares in Blue and a cash payment of £99,000.
Blue plc is to redeem its own debentures at par.

ORANGE plc   All the assets and liabilities except the bank overdraft to be taken over at a price of £98,000, half of the purchase price to be in ordinary shares in Rainbow.

GREEN plc   Rainbow will not take over the creditors but will take over all the assets, including bank, and will settle with one ordinary share in Rainbow for each ordinary share in Green. The debenture holders are to receive 200 ordinary shares in Rainbow for every £100 debentures. £25,000 is to be paid to Green in cash.

All the necessary formalities are completed by 31 May 1986 by which time Rainbow plc have issued all the remaining shares at a premium of 5p per share. Legal expenses of the take-over, £20,000, have been paid and land and buildings have been revalued at £100,000. Apart from this there are no other transactions for Rainbow for the month.

The following are the summarised balance sheets of the three companies at 30 April 1986:

	Blue plc £000s	Orange plc £000s	Green plc £000s
Goodwill	–	36	8
Land and Buildings	40	12	–
Plant and Machinery	44	20	12
Other fixed assets	25	10	5
Stocks	66	30	20
Debtors	120	90	18
Bank	50	(25) credit	4
Creditors	(80)	(70)	(6)
	265	103	61

Ordinary Shares of £1 each	110	108	50
8% Preference Shares of £1 each	60	–	–
6% Debentures	70	–	8
Reserves	12	–	1
Retained Profits	13	(5) debit	2
	265	103	61

You are required to:

(a) Show the realisation accounts, sundry shareholders' accounts and bank accounts in the books of the three selling companies.

(b) Show the Journal entry to record the takeover of the three companies in the books of Rainbow plc.

(c) Draw up the Balance Sheet of Rainbow plc at 31 May 1986.

IGNORE TAXATION $[40]$

(OLE)

Solution 7.1

(a)

Blue plc

Realisation

		£			£
Apr. 30	Land and buildings	40,000	Apr. 30	Creditors	80,000
	Plant and machinery	44,000		Rainbow plc [Working 1]	168,900
	Other fixed assets	25,000		Sundry shareholders	46,100
	Stocks	66,000			
	Debtors	120,000			
		295,000			295,000

Bank

Apr. 30	Balance b/d	50,000	Apr. 30	Debentures	70,000
	Rainbow plc	99,000		Sundry shareholders	79,000
		149,000			149,000

Sundry shareholders

Apr. 30	Realisation	46,100	Apr. 30	Ordinary shares	110,000
	Bank	79,000		Reserves	12,000
	Rainbow plc	9,900		Retained profits	13,000
		135,000			135,000

Rainbow plc*

Apr. 30	Realisation	168,900	Apr. 30	Sundry shareholders	9,900
				Preference shareholders	60,000
				Bank	99,000
		168,900			168,900

61

WORKING 1

		£
Shares to ordinary shareholders, ratio 9:50, is 19,800 @ 50p		9,900
Shares to preference shareholders, ratio 4:2, is 120,000 @ 50p		60,000
Cash		99,000
		168,900

*Not required by question but shown here for illustrative purposes.

Orange plc

Realisation

		£			£
Apr. 30	Land and buildings	12,000	Apr. 30	Creditors	70,000
	Plant and machinery	20,000		Rainbow plc	98,000
	Other fixed assets	10,000			
	Stocks	30,000			
	Debtors	90,000			
	Sundry shareholders	6,000			
		168,000			168,000

Bank

Apr. 30	Rainbow plc	49,000	Apr. 30	Balance b/d	25,000
				Sundry shareholders	24,000
		49,000			49,000

Sundry shareholders

Apr. 30	Goodwill	36,000	Apr. 30	Ordinary shares	108,000
	Retained profits	5,000		Realisation	6,000
	Bank	24,000			
	Rainbow plc	49,000			
		114,000			114,000

Green plc

Realisation

Apr. 30	Plant and machinery	12,000	Apr. 30	Rainbow plc [Working 2]	58,000
	Other fixed assets	5,000		Sundry shareholders	1,000
	Stocks	20,000			
	Debtors	18,000			
	Bank	4,000			
		59,000			59,000

Bank

Apr. 30	Balance b/d	4,000	Apr. 30	Realisation	4,000
	Green plc	25,000		Creditors	6,000
				Sundry shareholders	19,000
		29,000			29,000

Sundry shareholders

Apr. 30			Apr. 30		
Goodwill	8,000		Ordinary shares	50,000	
Rainbow plc	25,000		Reserves	1,000	
Realisation	1,000		Retained profits	2,000	
Bank	19,000				
	53,000			53,000	

WORKING 2

	£
Shares to ordinary shareholders, ratio 1:1, is 50,000 @ 50p =	25,000
Shares to debenture holders, ratio 200:100, is 16,000 @ 50p =	8,000
Cash	25,000
	58,000

(b)

	Blue Dr. £	Blue Cr £	Orange Dr. £	Orange Cr. £	Green Dr. £	Green Cr. £
Land and buildings	40,000		12,000			
Plant and machinery	44,000		20,000		12,000	
Other fixed costs	25,000		10,000		5,000	
Stock	66,000		30,000		20,000	
Debtors	120,000		90,000		18,000	
Bank					4,000	
Creditors		80,000		70,000		
Blue plc		168,900				
Capital reserve		46,100				1,000
Orange plc				98,000		
Goodwill			6,000			
Green plc						58,000
	295,000	295,000	168,000	168,000	59,000	59,000

Acquisition of businesses of Blue, Orange and Green

(c)

Rainbow plc: Balance Sheet as at 3 May 1986

	£	£
Fixed assets		
Intangible assets: Goodwill		6,000
Tangible assets: Lands and buildings	100,000	
Plant and machinery	76,000	
Other	40,000	216,000
		222,000
Current assets		
Stock	116,000	
Debtors	228,000	
Bank*	193,910	
	537,910	
less Creditors amounts falling due within one year	150,000	
Net Current assets		387,910
Total Assets less Current liabilities		£609,910
Capital and reserves		
Ordinary shares 50p		500,000
Share premium*		34,810
Revaluation reserve		48,000
Capital reserve [£47,100 − £20,000]		27,100
		£609,910
* As taken over		4,000
Issue of remaining shares 696,200 @ 55p		382,910
		386,910
less Cash paid on takeover of Blue, Orange and Green	173,000	
Legal expenses	20,000	193,000
		193,910

Example 7.2

X, M and R are the only directors of Smartsell Ltd, a men's clothing retailer, each owning one-third of the shares of the company. The balance sheet of Smartsell Ltd as at 31 October 1984 is as follows:

	£	£	£
Fixed Assets			
Premises		20,000	
Fixtures		10,000	30,000
Current Assets			
Stock	8,000		
Debtors	3,000		
Cash	2,000	13,000	
less: Current Liabilities			
Creditors		4,000	9,000
			39,000
Authorised Capital 40,000 £1 ordinary shares			
Issued share capital 24,000 £1 ordinary shares			24,000
Profit and Loss Account			15,000
			39,000

In addition to his interest in Smartsell Ltd, X is in business as a sole trader manufacturing clothes for Smartsell and other retailers. The balance sheet of X as at 31 October 1984 is as follows:

	£	£	£
Fixed Assets			
Machinery			8,000
Current Assets			
Stock	5,000		
Debtors	4,000		
Cash	1,000	10,000	
less: Current Liabilities			
Creditors	2,000	2,000	8,000
			16,000
Capital			16,000

Profits for the two businesses over the last three years ended 31 October are as follows:

	1982	1983	1984
	£	£	£
Net profit X	6,000	11,000	10,000
Net profit Smartsell	26,000	30,000	28,000

It has been agreed that Smartsell Ltd will take over all of the assets and liabilities of X at their balance sheet valuation on the following basis.

(1) The purchase price of the business of X will be twice the average profit of the business for the past three years. X will receive £10,000 cash, which he will invest outside the business at 10 per cent per annum, and 4,000 ordinary shares in Smartsell Ltd in full consideration of the purchase price.

(2) M and R have agreed to purchase for cash 4,000 shares each on the same valuation as the shares issued to X.

(3) After the takeover, the following revaluations of assets will take place: fixtures £8,000, stock £7,000.

REQUIRED

(a) The balance sheet of Smartsell Ltd immediately after the takeover is completed.

[*13 marks*]

(b) Assuming that profits for Smartsell Ltd for the next three years will average the same as over the last three years, calculate the difference in total income accruing to X as a result of the merger.

[*7 marks*]

(AEB)

Solution 7.2

(a)

	£
Average profits of X for last 3 years [£27,000 ÷ 3]	9,000
Value of business 2 × £9,000	18,000
Net book value of assets less liabilities	16,000
Amount paid for goodwill [£18,000 − £16,000]	2,000

Consideration is made up of cash £10,000 and shares £8,000 (£18,000 − £10,000). Nominal value of shares is £4,000; therefore premium of £4,000 (£8,000 as above, less £4,000 nominal value). Additional shares therefore also issued at premium of £1.

Smartsell Ltd: Balance Sheet as at 31 October 1984

	£	£
Fixed assets		
Intangible − Goodwill		2,000
Tangible − Premises	20,000	
Machinery	8,000	
Fixtures	8,000	36,000
		38,000
Current assets		
Stock	12,000	
Debtors	7,000	
Cash*	9,000	
	28,000	
less Creditors amounts falling due within one year	6,000	
Net Current assets		22,000
Total Assets less Current liabilities		56,000
Capital and reserves		
Authorised 40,000 £1 ordinary shares		
Issued 36,000 £1 ordinary shares		36,000
Share premium		12,000
Profit and loss account (£15,000 − £3,000)		12,000
		56,000

*£2,000 (Smartsell) + £1,000 (X) + £16,000 (8,000 additional shares at £2 each) − £10,000 (cash to X)

(b)

X currently earns:

	£
$\frac{1}{3} \times$ average Smartsell profits (£28,000)	9,333
average MR profits	9,000
	18,333

Under the new set-up, X will receive $\frac{1}{3}$ of the profits of the combined business, which are assumed to remain unchanged — i.e. £12,333 [$\frac{1}{3} \times$ (£28,000 + £9,000)]. However, X's income will increase by £1,000 (10% × £10,000), resulting from cash compensation for his business, making £13,333 in total, which is £5,000 less than present earnings.

7.5 Further exercises

Question 7.1

The balance sheet as at 31 October 1985 of the partnership of Price and Williams is as follows:

	£	£		£	£
Capital Accounts			Fixed Assets		
Price	12,000		Premises	12,000	
Williams	9,000	21,000	Fixtures	5,000	17,000
Current Account			Current Assets		
Price	8,000		Stock	4,000	
Williams	(2,000)		Debtors	6,000	
		6,000	Cash	3,000	13,000
Current Liabilities					
Creditors		3,000			
		30,000			30,000

The profits of the partnership for the years ended 31 October 1984 and 31 October 1985 were £20,000 and £30,000, respectively. The partners share the profits equally.

The partners have received an offer from Z Company Ltd for the takeover of the partnership business which would be valued at twice the average annual profit over the last two years, the consideration being 100,000 50p ordinary shares in Z Company Ltd. The shareholders in Z Company Ltd at present earn a dividend of 10p per share and the directors believe that this level of dividend can be maintained. Both Price and Williams will be offered two-year consultancy posts with Z Company Ltd with a salary of £6,000 per annum each. If they decide to accept the offer, the partners have agreed that the shares would be divided in two stages: firstly, to settle their individual balances on capital and current accounts in the partnership as at 31 October 1985; secondly, any remaining shares would be distributed equally. Z Company Ltd wish to use the takeover as an opportunity to revalue the premises up to the maximum value possible without having to create a revaluation reserve. The balance sheet as at 31 October 1985 of Z Company Ltd is as follows:

	£		£	£
Authorised Capital		Fixed Assets		
300,000 ordinary share @ 50p each	150,000	Fixtures	25,000	
		Motor vehicles	15,000	40,000
Issued Capital		Current Assets		
140,000 ordinary shares @ 50p each		Stock	20,000	
fully paid	70,000	Debtors	18,000	
Reserves		Cash	7,000	45,000
Share premium	5,000			
Current Liabilities				
Creditors	10,000			
	85,000			85,000

REQUIRED

(a) Advise Price and Williams whether they should accept the offer from Z Company Ltd. (Answers should include appropriate computations; non-financial considerations should be taken into account.) [17 marks]

(b) The balance sheet of Z Company Ltd immediately after the proposed takeover. [8 marks]

(AEB)

Answer 7.1

(a)

The average annual profit is £25,000 [(£30,000 + £20,000) ÷ 2]. The business, therefore, is valued at £50,000 [2 × £25,000].

The partners would receive shares as follows:

	Price	*Williams*
	£	£
Settlement of capital and current account	20,000	7,000
equivalent to 50p shares	40,000	14,000
remainder split evenly	23,000	23,000
Total number of shares held	63,000	37,000
expected dividend @ 10p	6,300	3,700
add consultancy salary	6,000	6,000
	12,300	9,700

This compares with average earnings of £12,500 [£25,000 ÷ 2] each as partners of the business. Financially therefore, they would appear to do less well if they were to accept the offer. An advantage would be that they have a more secure income with less responsibility than if they were partners.

(b)

Z Company Ltd: Balance Sheet as at 31 October 1985

	£	£
Fixed assets		
Premises [Working 1]		35,000
Fixtures		30,000
Motor vehicles		15,000
		80,000
Current assets		
Stock	24,000	
Debtors	24,000	
Cash	10,000	
	58,000	
less Creditors amounts falling due within one year	13,000	
Net Current assets		45,000
Total Assets less Current liabilities		125,000
Capital and reserves		
50p Ordinary shares 240,000		120,000
Share premium		5,000
		125,000

WORKING 1

	£
Value of partnership assets less liabilities taken over	27,000
less amount at which partnership valued	50,000
maximum increase in value of premises	23,000

Question 7.2

A. Friend, a manufacturer, had prepared the following balance sheet as at 31 May 1985.

	£	£	Fixed Assets	£ Cost	£ Aggregate Depreciation	£ Net
Capital						
Opening balance		95,500				
Net profit for year		15,000	Premises	30,000	–	30,000
			Plant and machinery	25,000	13,000	12,000
		110,500	Motor vehicles	10,000	6,500	3,500
Less Drawings		12,000				
				65,000	19,500	45,500
		98,500				
Current Liabilities			Current Assets			
Trade creditors	28,000		Stock	40,000		
Accrued expenses	2,100	30,100	Trade debtors	26,500		
			Balance at bank	15,500		
			Cash	1,100		83,100
		128,600				128,600

Friend had recently received an offer from another businessman who wished to purchase the business. The terms of the offer were as follows.

(1) All current liabilities would be taken over at book value.
(2) The fixed assets would be re-valued as follows:
  – premises at £60,000,
  – plant and machinery to be written down by 20 per cent of book value and motor vehicles by 30 per cent of book value.
(3) Stock would be re-valued to £30,000.
(4) Bad debts of £1,500 were to be written off and a provision for doubtful debts of 10 per cent of the net debtors was to be created.
(5) The assets remaining were to be retained by Friend.
(6) The agreed purchase price was £120,000 and it was to be settled in cash.

REQUIRED

(a) Explain what is meant by a 'going concern' valuation of a business.   [*4 marks*]
(b) A concise statement indicating the accounting bases used by Friend for the valuation of
  (i) freehold premises
  (ii) plant and machinery
  (iii) stock.
  How would the valuation of each of these assets be affected if the business ceased to be regarded as a 'going concern'?   [*10 marks*]
(c) An accounting statement showing the amount of goodwill that the businessman is prepared to pay for the business.   [*6 marks*]
(d) What other factors would the businessman have considered before finally agreeing to buy the business?   [*5 marks*]
            (AEB)

Answer 7.2

(a) Refer to Chapter 1: a continuing operation.
(b) (i) Market value of similar properties.
   (ii) Replacement cost less provision for depreciation.
   (iii) Lower of cost and net realisable value.

   Values would need to be revised to a realisable value if the business was considered not to be a 'going concern'.
(c) Assets to be taken over at revalued amounts:

	£	£
Fixed assets		
Premises		60,000
Plant and machinery [£12,000 – 20%]		9,600
Motor vehicles [£3,500 – 30%]		2,450
		72,050
Current assets		
Stock	30,000	
Debtors [(£26,500 – £1,500) – 10%]	22,500	
	52,500	
less Current liabilities	30,100	
		22,400
Net Assets		94,450

The amount paid for goodwill is therefore £120,000 less £94,450 – i.e. £25,550.
(d) Prospects of business, order book. Age of fixed assets – When will they need replacing? Is Friend likely to set up as a competitor?

8 Capital Reconstruction

8.1 The need for capital reconstruction

Capital reconstruction schemes usually become necessary following periods of losses, and any or all of the following features will be present.

(i) A debit balance will have built up on the profit and loss account.
(ii) In addition to (i), there may be other debit balances on the books, representing a non-existent or fictitious asset – e.g. goodwill.
(iii) The business may be unable to meet its obligations to creditors as and when payments become due. These obligations will include interest relating to loans.
(iv) There may be arrears of dividends on cumulative preference shares.

8.2 The object of the reconstruction

A company suffering from the above symptoms will find it very difficult, if not impossible, to raise new finance. This will make it very difficult to continue trading; in fact, the obvious action may seem to be to wind up the company. Winding up is obviously a drastic step, and a business will usually make every attempt to avoid it. If winding up is to be avoided, what the company really needs is a fresh start, and this is where the capital reconstruction scheme comes in.

The primary objectives of the scheme must be to:

(i) eliminate non-existent or fictitious assets from the balance sheet;
(ii) restate other assets to more realistic values if necessary (for example, stocks may need restating to realisable values and provision may be required against bad or doubtful debts).

8.3 How the reconstruction is achieved

The easy part will usually be deciding the values at which assets should be restated. However, this can only be achieved by a reduction in liabilities or capital or reserves. The first reaction of a creditor will be: why should I accept a scheme which offers me less than I am due? Similarly, a shareholder would ask why he should accept a reduction in the value (albeit the nominal value) of the shares he owns. The answer to both is that by accepting the scheme they will benefit more than by allowing the company to go into liquidation.

Consequently, a reconstruction, after much negotiation, will usually be achieved along all or any of the following lines.

(i) Creditors (including debenture holders) may accept newly issued shares in lieu of part or all of the amounts owed to them. Alternatively, they may forego part of the debt altogether.

(ii) Preference shareholders may agree to forego arrears on dividends. They may also accept a reduction in the value of their shares, or the issue of new shares (of a lesser value) in replacement of their existing shares.

(iii) Ordinary shareholders, because they would receive less in a winding up, must also be prepared to take the majority of the writing down in any reconstruction scheme. As in (ii), this may be achieved by reducing the nominal value of the shares held or cancelling the existing shares and issuing new ones of a lesser value.

The negotiations to achieve the above will often be long and arduous. Once everybody (sometimes only a majority) is in agreement there are then legal requirements which have to be observed. However, any examination question on this topic will be mostly, if not wholly, concerned with the accounting treatment of the reconstruction.

8.4 The reconstruction account

The reconstruction account is at the centre of the accounting treatment, which we will now illustrate.

(i) Transfer to the reconstruction account any debit balances to be written off or eliminated by

    Dr. Reconstruction
    Cr. Asset (or profit and loss where we need to eliminate the debit balance on that account)

Where any asset is only partially being written down, then the above entry will be for the amount of the reduction only.

(ii) Transfer to the reconstruction account the amount of any shares which are being cancelled, or the value by which they are being reduced, as follows:

    Dr. Share capital
    Cr. Reconstruction

Where shares are issued in replacement, then

    Dr. Reconstruction
    Cr. Share capital

(iii) Transfer to the reconstruction account the amount of any liabilities being foregone by

    Dr. Liability
    Cr. Reconstruction

If shares are issued as part of the scheme, then record as in (ii) above.

(iv) Deal with any remaining balance on the reconstruction account as required
– for example,

> Dr./Cr. Reconstruction
> Dr./Cr   Reserves

8.5 Worked example

Example 8.1

The Anglo Stock plc has been trading as a retailer for a number of years, but has recently been having difficulty in trading. In order to make the company more attractive a scheme for restructuring the capital of the company has been agreed by all the necessary parties involved, with effect from 1 January 1984.

At 31 December 1983, the following were some of the items appearing in the balance sheet:

	£
Issued Share Capital – 8% Preference Shares of £1	200,000
Ordinary Shares of £1	1,200,000
Capital Reserves	113,000
Revenue Reserves	20,000
Profit and Loss Account (debit balance)	820,000
10% Loan Stock	150,000
Fixed Assets (Book value)	1,618,000
Stock	80,000
Trade Debtors	20,000
Bank	5,000
Trade Creditors	40,000
Loan Stock Interest Owing	15,000

NOTE

The preference dividend has not been paid since 31 December 1980.

The terms of the reconstruction have been agreed as follows;

(a) The nominal value of the ordinary shares shall be reduced to 40p each.
(b) The preference shares shall be cancelled and replaced by a 3 for 4 issue of new 10 per cent Preference shares redeemable in 2005. The nominal value of the shares is £1.
(c) The Preference dividend outstanding will be honoured by the issue of Ordinary shares to the preference shareholders.
(d) The creditors will be offered settlement by a payment of 50p in the £ and new ordinary shares to the balance. Three-quarters of the creditors accept this offer; the remainder are paid in full.
(e) Sufficient Ordinary Shares shall be issued at 50p, payable in full on application, to bring the issued share capital to its original value. This issue was fully subscribed and the shares were allotted on 25 February 1984.
(f) The Capital reserves are to be utilised before revenue reserves are used.
(g) The loan stock interest outstanding is settled by a cash payment.

During the year ending 31 December 1984 the company modernised their retail outlets at a capital cost of £400,000, half of which had been paid by 31 December. Business was boosted by an original advertising campaign which was to be repeated in 1985. The total cost of the campaign was £50,000 and all of this was paid in 1984.

Receipts from Debtors during the year were £1,240,000 and £1,570,000 was paid to creditors and for operating expenses.

The company made profits for the year of £75,000 (after tax and appropriations). Depreciation of £309,000 had been charged; the preference dividend had been paid as had the Loan Stock interest. £10,000 had been transferred to reserves.

Apart from any balances which can be ascertained from above, the following appeared in the books at 31 December 1984:

	£
Stock	67,000
Trade Debtors	25,000
Trade Creditors	18,000

You are required to prepare:

(i) Journal entries for the items (a) to (g) above, [22]

(ii) A summarised Bank account for the year ending 31 December 1984, [9]

(iii) A summarised Balance Sheet at 31 December 1984. [9]

[Total 40]

(OLE)

Solution 8.1

(i)

	Dr.	Cr.
	£	£
(a) Ordinary share capital	720,000	
Capital reduction		720,000

Reduction in nominal value of 1,200,000 shares from £1 to 40p

(b) 8% Preference share capital	200,000	
Capital reduction		200,000

Cancellation of preference shares

Capital reduction	150,000	
10% Preference share capital		150,000

Issue of redeemable preference shares

(c) Capital reduction	48,000	
Ordinary share capital		48,000

Issue of 120,000 ordinary shares of 40p to preference shareholders in lieu of arrears of preference share dividends

(d) Creditors	30,000	
Ordinary share capital		15,000
Bank		15,000

Issue of 37,500 ordinary shares to creditors and 50% payment of outstanding debt in cash

Creditors	10,000	
Bank		10,000

Settlement of creditors not accepting ordinary shares

(e) Bank   883,750

	£	£
(e) Bank	883,750	
Ordinary share capital [Working 1]		707,000
Share premium		176,750

Issue of ordinary shares

WORKING 1

	£	£
Reduction as in (a) above		720,000
Reduction as in (b) above [£200,000 − £150,000]		50,000
		770,000
less increase as in (c) above	48,000	
increase as in (d) above	15,000	63,000
		707,000

	£	£
(f) Profit and Loss		820,000
Reconstruction	820,000	

Write off debit balance on profit and loss account

	£	£
Capital reserves	98,000	
Reconstruction		98,000

Write off balance remaining on reconstruction account after above entries

	£	£
(g) Interest	15,000	
Bank		15,000

Payment of outstanding loan interest

(ii)

(i

Bank

		£			£
Jan. 1	Balance b/d	5,000	Jan. 1	Creditors	15,000
	Ordinary shares	883,750		Creditors	10,000
	Debtors	1,240,000		Interest	15,000
			Dec. 31	Property	200,000
				Advertising	50,000
				Creditors	1,570,000
				Preference dividend	15,000
				Interest	15,000
				Bal c/d	238,750
		2,128,750			2,128,750

(iii)

Anglo Stock plc: Balance Sheet as at 31 December 1984

	£	£	£
Fixed Assets [Working 2]			1,709,000
Current Assets			
Stock		67,000	
Debtors		25,000	
Prepayment		25,000	
Bank		238,750	
		355,750	
less Creditors amounts falling due within one year			
Trade creditors	18,000		
Creditor for modernisation	200,000	218,000	
Net Current Assets			137,750
Total Assets less Current liabilities			1,846,750
less Creditors amounts falling due after more than one year: 10% Loan stock			150,000
			1,696,750
Capital – Reserves			
Issued share capital – 40p Ordinary shares			1,250,000
– £1 Preference shares			150,000
			1,400,000
Share premium			176,750
Capital reserves			15,000
Revenue reserves			30,000
Profit and loss account			75,000
			1,696,750

WORKING 2	£
As given	1,618,000
addition	400,000
	2,018,000
less depreciation	309,000
	1,709,000

8.6 Further exercise

Question 8.1

The following information was available on Andando Ltd as at 31 December 1984.

	£
Net profit for year	300,000
Trade creditors	70,000
9% £1 preference shares, fully paid	75,000
Retained earnings 1 January 1984	250,000
Share premium account	150,000
£1 ordinary shares, fully paid	500,000
General reserve	200,000
Revaluation of property reserve	500,000
Interim preference share dividend paid	3,375

All the authorised ordinary share capital, but only three-quarters of the authorised preference share capital, had been issued.

After a review of the company's financial position the directors had approved a scheme to change the capital structure of the company.

(1) The revised authorised capital for which approval had been obtained was:

   3,000,000 £1 ordinary shares
   250,000 9% £1 preference shares.

(2) An issue of bonus shares was made on the basis of two shares for every one ordinary share held. Funds for the issue were appropriated as follows:

	£
Transfer from the share premium account	150,000
Transfer from the revaluation of property reserve	500,000

The balance required was taken from total retained earnings.
The shares were issued on 31 December 1984, but would not qualify for dividend until December 1985.

(3) In order to increase cash funds an issue of debentures was made on 1 January 1985. The terms of the issue were:
£200,000 8% Debenture stock 1996–2000 issued at £98 for £100 of debenture stock, cash payable on issue.

In addition the company's accountant discovered that the following items had not been entered into the company's books.

(4) A substantial trade debtor owing £50,000 had gone into liquidation on 1 December 1984. The receiver had advised the company that unsecured creditors would not receive any money.

(5) The directors had recommended dividend payments as follows:
   ordinary shareholders: 10p a share
   preference shareholders: 9% for the year, but the first half year payment of $4\frac{1}{2}$% had already been paid.

(6) On 28 December 1984 £7,000 of goods bought on credit for stock had been included in the year end stock valuation, but no entry had been made in the purchases day book.

REQUIRED

(a) Journal entries to record
   (i) the changed capital structure
   (ii) the year end adjustments.
   (Narratives are not required.)   [*9 marks*]
(b) A balance sheet extract as at 1 January 1985, showing only the content of the shareholders' total interest.   [*8 marks*]
(c) Explain what benefits accrue to an ordinary shareholder on receipt of the bonus shares
   (i) in the short run
   (ii) in the long run.   [*5 marks*]
(d) A list showing **three** of the components of the shareholders' total interest in a limited company which the Companies Acts require to be published as separate items.[*3 marks*]

(AEB)

Answer 8.1

(a)

(i)

	Dr.	Cr.
	£	£
Share premium	150,000	
Revaluation of property reserve	500,000	
Retained earnings	350,000	
Ordinary share capital		1,000,000
Bank	196,000	
Discount on debentures	4,000	
Debenture stock		200,000

(ii)

Profit and loss	50,000	
Trade debtors		50,000
Dividends payable (Profit and loss)	53,375	
Dividends payable (Balance sheet)		53,375
Purchases	7,000	
Profit and loss		7,000

(b)

Authorised share capital:		
3,000,000 £1 ordinary shares		3,000,000
250,000 £1 9% preference shares		250,000
		3,250,000
Issued share capital:		
1,500,000 £1 ordinary shares		1,500,000
75,000 £1 9% preference shares		75,000
		1,575,000
General reserve		200,000
Profit and loss account [Working 1]		82,250
		1,857,250

WORKING 1

	£	£
As given at 1 January 1984		250,000
add Net profit for year	300,000	
Adjustment for bad debts	(50,000)	
Write off discount on debentures	(4,000)	
Cost of sales adjustment (purchases)	(7,000)	
		239,000
		489,000
less Utilised on issue of bonus shares		350,000
		139,000
less Dividends paid + proposed		(56,750)
		82,250

(c) Refer to Section 3.6. No real benefit accrues, since the shareholder now owns
more shares but with a lesser value. Theoretically, the shares may therefore be
easier to sell.

(d) Refer to Section 4.2.

9 Social Accounting

9.1 What is it?

Social accounting has been defined as 'the measurement and reporting, internal or external, of information concerning the impact of an entity and its activities on society'. It is, therefore, concerned with the reporting in accounting statements of a business's activities which affect society. Fundamental to its being is the idea that management's objectives should not solely be the maximisation of profits. They have additional responsibilities, such as:

   (i) to produce safe and reliable products of a high quality;
  (ii) to ensure that they do not cause pollution;
 (iii) to ensure that they do not discriminate against groups of workers such as women and ethnic minorities;
 (iv) to ensure that their employees are not exposed to undue risk;
  (v) to devote some effort towards social programmes.

9.2 The need and demand

(a) Internal

Under this heading we consider directors, management, other employees, local union, public relations department and legal department. In order to ensure that the business's policies are followed and that they are acknowledging their social responsibilities, all of the above need information. Such information might include, for example:

   (i) details of product testing, to ensure that there is no danger to consumer health, as well as details of any reported health risk or damage;
  (ii) the number of internal promotions and recruitments of women and from minority groups;
 (iii) details of energy usage and conservation efforts;
 (iv) details of the effects on the environment of the business's production systems and end products.

(b) External

Here we are concerned with the following:

   (i) investors and creditors;
  (ii) customers;
 (iii) suppliers;

(iv) government (e.g. Inland Revenue, Central Statistics Office, Department of Trade and Industry, etc.);

(v) public interest groups;

(vi) news media;

(vii) Stock exchanges, in the case of public companies.

9.3 Uses of social accounting

The users listed in Section 9.2 will in various ways use information produced, as follows:

(i) To ensure that legal requirements are met.

(ii) To ensure that a business's stated policies are followed.

(iii) To bring pressure on businesses to act in a socially responsible manner. This pressure may be directly on the business itself or indirectly via the Government or by other methods.

9.4 Worked examples

Example 9.1

Name four likely users of accounting statements of a Public Limited Company, stating in each case what you consider to be the most significant piece of information they would look for. (OLE)

Solution 9.1

Refer to the text. Shareholders: profit. Trade creditors: liquidity. Labour force: forward outlook in so far as it affects employment prospects. Loan creditors: interest cover.

Example 9.2

Fastfreeze Ltd completed its third year in business as a manufacturer of frozen foods on 31 May 1985. Although selling a wide range of products, 'Icepeel', a frozen pudding, for young children has been particularly successful. 'Icepeel' is made from a variety of ingredients and mixed in a special machine. Two problems concerning the production of 'Icepeel' are facing the company.

(1) The special machine used for mixing 'Icepeel' was purchased on 1 June 1982 at a cost of £16,000 and now needs replacing. Installation costs of £4,000 were incurred in June 1982 and in addition a service contract was entered into for the life of the machine at a cost of £1,000 per annum. A replacement machine will cost £30,000 plus £5,000 installation costs and will require no service agreement. The existing machine has a trade-in value of £3,000. It is company policy to use the reducing balance method of depreciation at a rate of 20 per cent per annum.

(2) An article in a leading medical journal has claimed that one of the ingredients used in the production of 'Icepeel' causes excessive decay in children's teeth.

(a) The provision for depreciation account for each of the three years ended 31 May 1983, 1984 and 1985. [5 marks]
(b) A statement showing the total charge against profits in the financial year ending 31 May 1986 if the replacement machine were to be purchased on 31 December 1985. [4 marks]
(c) Define depreciation and outline the factors to be considered in the determination of a depreciation policy. [7 marks]
(d) A critical examination of the factors that Fastfreeze Ltd should consider in deciding whether to continue to produce 'Icepeel'. [7 marks]

(AEB)

Solution 9.2

(a)

Provision for depreciation

		£			£
1983 May 31	Balance c/d	4,000	1983 May 31 Profit and loss [Note 1]		4,000
1984 May 31	Balance c/d	7,200	1983 June 1 Balance b/d		4,000
			1984 May 31 Profit and loss [Note 2]		3,200
		7,200			7,200
1985 May 31	Balance c/d	9,760	1984 June 1 Balance b/d		7,200
			1985 May 31 Profit and loss [Note 3]		2,560
		9,760			9,760

NOTES

(1) 20% × (£16,000 + £4,000).
(2) 20% × (£20,000 − £4,000).
(3) 20% × (£20,000 − £7,200). Alternatively, it could be argued that, since the machine is in need of replacement, it should be written down to its realisable value.

(b)

	£
Net book value at 1 June 1985 [£20,000 − £9,760]	10,240
Sale proceeds	3,000
Loss on disposal of machinery	7,240
Depreciation of machinery 20% × (£30,000 + £5,000)	7,000
Total charge against profits	14,240

(c) Depreciation is defined in SSAP12 as 'a measure of wearing out, consumption or other loss of value of a fixed asset whether arising from use, effluxion of time or obsolescence through technology and market change'.

The 1985 Companies Act states: '. . .any fixed asset which has a limited useful economic life. . . shall be reduced by provisions for depreciation calculated to write off that amount systematically over the period of the asset's useful economic life'. The factors to be considered are therefore:

(i) Cost, including expenses incidental to acquisition.
(ii) Estimated useful economic life.

(iii) Estimated residual value.

(iv) Depreciation method — e.g. straight line or reducing balance.

(d) Refer to the text. The company has a difficulty in that there is conflict between its responsibility to shareholders to earn profit, to the labour force to provide employment and to society to act in a socially responsible way. The company has an obligation to ascertain the validity of the claim in the medical journal; this may involve conducting its own research or employing an outside agency to do it.

9.5   Further exercises

Question 9.1

'The cost of obtaining data should not exceed the benefits to be gained from having it.' Explain with examples what this statement means.

Answer 9.1

Refer to the text. Information is an aid to decision-making; therefore do not spend more in gathering it than profit which can be earned from using it. Difficulty occurs with measuring benefit from disclosures designed to ensure that the company is acting responsibly.

Question 9.2

Tenido Limited had appointed a new managing director and at his request the company's accountant produced the following financial information for the year ended 30 June 1986.

Revenue Statement for the
year ended 30 June 1986

	£	£
Sales		650,000
less Cost of goods sold		400,000
Gross profit		250,000
Administration expenses	70,000	
Selling and distribution expenses	80,000	150,000
Net profit		100,000

The accountant also provided the following information.

(1) The accountant normally valued stock at cost but he had decided to value the closing stock on 30 June 1986 at market price, as the company was applying for a bank loan. In his view the company's financial position should be presented favourably.

The closing stock cost valuation was £50,000 (market price valuation, £80,000).

(2) The accountant had always ensured that the company paid its expense bills as soon as they arrived in order that there should be no outstanding creditors.

At 30 June 1985 the following bills had been paid and wholly charged to the 1984/85 profit and loss account:

(i) £1,500 for rent covering the period from 1 April 1985 to 30 September 1985.

(ii) £1,000 for a press advertising campaign which commenced on 1 June 1985 and ended on 31 July 1985.

During June 1986, a bill of £800 was paid for miscellaneous items of stationery. On 30 June 1986, a stock of £530 of the stationery remained. The 1985/86 revenue statement had been charged with £800.

None of the remaining expense items covered any part of another accounting period.

(3) The sales figure for the year included £20,000 for goods sent to customers on a sale or return basis. Customers were debited with the cost price plus 25 per cent. None of these goods had been confirmed as sales as at 30 June 1986.

The new managing director advised the company's accountant that he was not satisfied with many aspects of the accounting policies currently pursued, and that he wanted the Revenue Statement for the year ended 30 June 1986 revised.

He also advised the accountant that in the future he intends to consider social aspects of accounting whenever it appears as a relevant factor.

REQUIRED

(a) A revised revenue statement for the year ended 30 June 1986, based on normally accepted accounting principles rather than the accounting policies pursued by the accountant. *[10 marks]*

(b) A brief description of the accounting principles used as the basis for the adjustments made in your revised revenue statement. *[8 marks]*

(c) A concise statement explaining what the managing director means by the social aspects of accounting. Give **three** examples of factors which would be considered as social accounting. *[7 marks]*

(AEB)

Answer 9.2

(a) Adjustments required:
   (1) Reduce closing stock and thus increase cost of sales by £30,000.
   (2) 1984/5 expenses should have been £1,250 less (£750 rent and £500 advertising). 1985/6 expenses are therefore understated by £1,250 (as above) and overstated by £530 in respect of stationery stock.
   (3) Reduce sales by £20,000. Increase finished stocks by £16,000 and thus decrease cost of sales by £16,000.

(b) (1) Matching concept, cost concept.
   (2) Matching concept.
   (3) Prudence concept.

(c) Refer to the text.

10 Branch Accounts

10.1 Introduction

Many retailing and wholesaling companies operate from more than one site. These other locations are known as branches. Among many well-known examples might be mentioned such companies as Tesco, Sainsbury, and Marks and Spencer.

The system of accounting falls into two categories:

(i) where the head office of the company keeps all the accounting records (except branch cash, branch debtors);
(ii) where the branches operate their own full set of accounting records, as if they were a separate business entity.

We shall look at both of these systems.

10.2 Head office keeps all accounting records

Under this system there are two main accounts which must be prepared in order for the head office to determine the profit or loss made by each branch. They are: (a) the branch stock account; (b) the branch adjustment account.

The *branch stock account* shows all movement of stock into and out of the branch. Quite often, after allowing for opening and closing stock, the account will not balance. This is usually because of 'missing' stock. One of the prime purposes of the account is to determine the amount of 'missing' stock. If this is abnormally high, head office can initiate an inquiry into the branch activities.

Usually the branch stock account shows all stock at the branch selling price. This makes it easier for head office, which controls prices, to monitor stock movements. The following account shows the typical debit and credit entries for a branch stock account.

Branch stock account (at branch sales prices)

Opening stock b/d	: Sales
Goods from head office	: Returns to head office
Returns in	: Closing stock c/d
	: Damaged stock
	: 'Missing' stock

In most examination questions, the head office uses a mark-up when determining the prices which the branch should charge to its customers. You must be familiar with the relationship between gross mark-ups and gross margin when dealing with branch accounts (see Chapter 12).

The main function of the *branch adjustment account* is to determine the gross profit earned by the branch. We credit the branch adjustment account with the maximum gross profit it could have made during the period, and debit the account with the reasons why it did not achieve that profit. Obviously, the balance is the gross profit/loss for the period.

Branch adjustment account

Total sales value of missing stock:	Gross profit in opening stock ⎫ Maximum
Total sales value of damaged stock:	Gross profit in goods from H/O ⎭ profit
Gross profit in returns to H/O:	
Gross profit in closing stock:	
Balance = branch gross profit	

10.3 Branches keep independent accounting records

Profit and loss accounts of branches and for the company's overall results are normally required where independent records are kept by branches. There are several major rules to adhere to when compiling the profit and loss accounts.

(i) There will be a trading, profit and loss account for each branch. These are compiled from the trial balance of each branch (with the usual year-end adjustments). The trading, profit and loss account *must* be compiled as though each branch were an independent business. This is because we are trying to calculate the net profit made by the branch in its own right.

(ii) There will be a trading, profit and loss account for the head office. Again this is compiled from the trial balance of the head office.

The sales of the head office will be made up of 'sales to branches' and 'sales' (i.e. sales to the public).

The purchases of the head office are made up of all purchases made by the head office, whether for head office use or for eventual use by the branches.

(iii) In the profit and loss account of the head office we must make an adjustment for the 'provision for unrealised profit': see Section 10.4.

(iv) There will be a trading, profit and loss account for the company as a whole. We must exclude any intercompany sales and intercompany purchases from the company trading account. Opening and closing stock must be valued at original cost to the company.

(v) The opening and closing stock of the company must include any 'goods in transit' — this is stock which has been sent by the head office to a branch or, vice versa, which has not arrived at its destination, and is therefore not included in the stock of the head office or the branch(es).

(vi) Apart from the adjustment for the provision for unrealised profit in the head office profit and loss account, the items in the *company* profit and loss account are simply the aggregate of figures in the head office and branches profit and loss account.

10.4 Provision for unrealised profit

Quite often the head office buys stock and then invoices it to the branches for more than the original cost to head office. This is because the head office itself is acting as a profit centre. If some of this stock is still unsold at the branch at the end of the year, there is an unrealised profit in their stock as far as the company profit is concerned. This unrealised profit must be deducted from head office net profit in the head office profit and loss account. (Credit provision for unrealised profit; debit head office profit and loss account.)

As with other provisions, in consecutive periods it is the change in the provision which will be debited or credited to the profit and loss account; the balance of the provision for unrealised profit at the end of the year is deducted from the aggregate stock valuation in the balance sheet for the company.

Example The head office buys stock and then sells it to the branch at a 25 per cent mark-up. At the start of the year the branch had stock from head office, which had been invoiced to the branch at £6,000. At the end of the year, the stock at the branch (from head office) was £9,000.

Provision for unrealised profit

	£			£	
		:	balance b/d	1,200	[(25/125) × £6,000]
		:	H/O Profit and loss	600	
Balance c/d [(25/125) × £9,000]	1,800				
	1,800	:		1,800	

H/O Profit and loss Account	:	
Gross profit		xxx
deduct Increase in provision for unrealised profits		600
deduct H/O Overheads		xxx
Net profit		xxx

Company balance Sheet (extract)

Current assets	£	
Stock	25,000	[aggregate of all stocks]
less Provision for unrealised profit	1,200	
	23,800	

10.5 Current accounts

To record how much money the head office has invested in a branch, the head office keeps a *branch current* account. This is debited with all monies or resources sent to the branch. It is credited with all remittances sent from the branch to the head office. This is similar to a debtors account. In head office books it would appear as follows:

Branch Current account

1. Fixed assets purchased for branch	:	Returns from branch
	:	Cash from branch
2. Goods sent to branch	:	
3. Overheads incurred by head office on behalf of branch	:	
4. Net profit	:	

The branch keeps a similar record of its indebtedness to the head office — also called a current account. Apart from the problem of time lags between items being sent and items being received, the balance of the branch current account in the head office books should agree with the head office current account in the branch books.

Current accounts are not shown in the company balance sheet.

There are two types of items in transit: (a) goods in transit; (b) cash in transit. The adjustment for these is usually made in the head office books *only*.

You must remember to include goods in transit in the company stock figure (deducting any unrealised profits). We also must include cash in transit in company current assets.

10.6 The balance sheet

Usually the only balance sheet required by examination questions is the one for the company as a whole.

The assets and liabilities are the simple aggregates of assets and liabilities of branches and head office, allowing for unrealised profit in closing stock.

The capital section of the balance sheet is made up of the capital (+ reserves) from the head office trial balance. The net profit of the branches is added to the net profit of the head office; if it is a limited company, the appropriation of profits, etc., is dealt with in the normal way, through the head office appropriation accounts.

10.7 Worked examples

Example 10.1

Cellgoods Ltd has a branch in Kidlington. All branch transactions are recorded in the head office books but the branch keeps a sales ledger and certain subsidiary books.

All purchases are made by the head office, goods being delivered direct to the branch and charged to it at selling price, which is cost plus 25 per cent.

On 1 January 1986 stock-in-trade at the branch, valued at selling price, amounted to £7,935 and the debtors to £2,061.

During the year ended 31 December 1986 the following transactions took place at the branch:

	£
Goods sent to branch at selling price	43,705
Goods returned to head office at selling price	820
Credit sales to customers	26,883
Returns from customers at selling price (items previously sold on credit)	616
Cash sales	13,142
Cash received from debtors	24,374
Discounts allowed	537
Bad debts written off	248

A consignment of goods despatched to the branch in December 1986 with a selling price of £300 was not received at the branch until January 1987. This item is included in the amount of goods sent to branches at selling price above, but has not been included in the stock figure.

At 31 December 1986 the stock-in-trade at the branch at selling price amounted to £11,030.

You are required to prepare:

(a) The branch stock account and branch total debtors account for the year ended 31 December 1986;

(b) A calculation of the branch gross profit.

(OLE)

Solution 10.1

Note: Sales margin = 20%; since the mark-up is 25% (on cost), the margin (profit/sales) = 25/(100 + 25).

Branch stock

	£		£
1.1.78 Bal b/d	7,935	Returns to h/o	820
Goods from h/o	43,705	Credit sales	26,883
Returns inwards	616	Cash sales	13,142
		Goods in transit	300
		Bal. c/d	11,030
		Missing stock	81
	52,256		52,256

Branch debtors

	£		£
1.1.78 Bal. b/d	2,061	Returns	616
Sales	26,883	Cash	24,374
		Discount allowed	537
		Bad debts	248
		Bal. c/d	3,169
	28,944		28,944

Branch adjustment

	£		£
Returns to h/o	164	Gross profit in o/stk	1,587
Missing stock	81	Goods from h/o	8,741
Gross profit c/stk	2,206		
Gross profit goods in transit	60		
Gross profit	7,817		
	10,328		10,328

Example 10.2

B. Wright is the owner of a small concern, Bi-rite, which has a Head Office, and branches in Oxford and Cambridge. All goods are purchased by Head Office and sent to branches and invoiced at cost to H.O. plus 20 per cent. The branches keep their own books and at the end of each year send to H.O. a trial balance from which the final accounts are prepared.

Below are the Trial Balances of Head Office and the two branches prepared at 31 May 1982.

Trial Balances at 31 May 1982

	Head Office		Oxford		Cambridge	
	£	£	£	£	£	£
Capital		200,000				
Premises	80,000		70,000		60,000	
Fixtures and fittings	40,000		30,000		20,000	
Motor vehicles	10,000					
Stocks at 1 June 1981	7,500		4,200		5,400	
Purchases	625,700					
Goods to branches at branch price		750,000	420,000		320,000	
Sales				495,000		400,200
General expenses	8,000		6,000		5,000	
Wages and salaries	40,000		4,000		3,000	
Selling expenses			12,000		9,000	
Carriage out	7,500		1,200		2,300	
Debtors and creditors	6,450	4,830	2,800	1,320	1,700	1,120
Bank	27,310		2,450		1,980	
Provision for unrealised profit		1,500				
Drawings	8,300					
Current account	63,530			56,330		
Current account	32,040					27,060
	956,330	956,330	552,650	552,650	428,380	428,380

NOTES

1. At 31 May 1982 stocks valued at cost H.O. £8,200. Stocks valued at cost to branches Oxford £3,120; Cambridge £3,260.
2. There are goods in transit at 31 May 1982 to Oxford £6,000 and to Cambridge £4,000.
3. Oxford and Cambridge have transferred to H.O. £1,200 and £980, respectively, which has not yet been entered in the H.O. books.
4. Wages and expenses paid by H.O. on behalf of branches during the year amounted to:

	Oxford	Cambridge
	£	£
Wages	20,000	15,000
Expenses	1,600	1,400

5. The carriage out incurred by H.O. is to be apportioned to Oxford and Cambridge in the proportion 3:2, respectively. Prepare the Trading and profit and loss accounts for the year ending 31 May 1982, showing the profit or loss made by H.O. and each branch, and the Balance Sheet of the business at the same date.

Show also the entries in the Oxford branch Current account at H.O. and explain what the balance represents. [40 marks]

(OLE)

Solution 10.2

Trading profit and loss for year ended 31 May 1982

	HEAD OFFICE		OXFORD		CAMBRIDGE	
	£	£	£	£	£	£
Sales		750,000		495,000		400,200
O/stock	7,500		4,200		5,400	
Purchases	625,700		420,000		320,000	
	633,200		424,200		325,400	
C/stock	8,200		3,120		3,260	
Cost of goods sold		625,000		421,080		322,140
Gross profit		125,000		73,920		78,060
Provision for unrealised profit	1,230					
General expenses	5,000		7,600		6,400	
Wages and salaries	5,000		24,000		18,000	
Selling expenses			12,000		9,000	
Carriage out			5,700		5,300	
		11,230		49,300		38,700
Net profit		113,770		24,620		39,360

Balance Sheet as at 31 May 1982

	£	£	£
Fixed assets			Net
Premises			210,000
Fixtures			90,000
Vehicles			10,000
			310,000
Current assets			
Stocks*	21,850		
Debtors	10,950		
Bank	31,740		
Cash in transit	2,180		
		66,720	
Current liabilities			
Creditors		7,270	
Working capital			59,450
Net assets			369,450
Financed by:			
Capital			200,000
Net profit			177,750
			377,750
Drawings			8,300
			369,450

WORKINGS

Provision for unrealised profit:

	£
Closing stock at branches	3,120
	3,260
Goods in transit	10,000
	16,380
Unrealised profit ($\frac{1}{6}$)	2,730
Old provision	1,500
Increase	1,230
Closing stocks	
At branches	6,380
In transit	10,000
	16,380
less Provision	2,730
	13,650
H.O. stock	8,200
	21,850
Opening stocks at branches	9,600
less Provision	1,500
	8,100
H.O.	7,500
	15,600

Oxford Current account

	£		£
Bal. b/d	63,530	Goods in transit	6,000
Wages	20,000	Cash in transit	1,200
Expenses	1,600	Bal. c/d	107,050
Carriage	4,500		
Net profit	24,620		
	114,250		114,250

The balance represents the branch's indebtedness to head office. It is equivalent to the company's investment in the branch.

10.8 Further exercise

Question 10.1

Hielo Ltd, a retail organisation, sells goods in three towns, Andarstown, Statford and Bington. Andarstown also provides the Head Office facilities of central buying, administration and warehousing. The following draft revenue statements, for the year ending 20 September 1985, had been prepared by Head Office.

	Statford		Bington		Andarstown	
	£	£	£	£	£	£
Sales		80,000		170,000		250,000
Opening stock	5,000		12,000		27,000	
Goods from Head Office	52,000		100,000		—	
Purchases	—		—		300,000	
					327,000	
Goods to branch					167,000	
	57,000		112,000		160,000	
Closing stock	7,000		18,000		15,000	
Cost of goods sold		50,000		94,000		145,000
Gross profit		30,000		76,000		105,000
Variable costs	20,000		25,000		30,000	
Fixed costs	15,000		18,000		22,000	
Allocation of Head Office costs	12,000	47,000	16,000	59,000	20,000	72,000
Profit/Loss		(17,000)		17,000		33,000

Additional information:

(1) At 30 September 1985 there were goods in transit but not yet received by the branches:

	£
Goods to Statford	5,000
Goods to Bington	10,000

(2) Branch managers receive, as an annual bonus, a commission of 1 per cent of gross sales, but the commission is reduced by any losses of stock at the branch. A manager is not expected to bear a stock loss greater than the total of the commission due.

(3) A year end audit on 30 September 1985 revealed stock losses as follows:

	£
Statford	1,000
Bington	900
Andarstown	1,500

No account had been taken of these stock losses in the preparation of the revenue statements above.

(4) Goods are invoiced to the branches at cost price.

(a) A statement showing the revised profit/loss for each of the trading branches after making allowance for the adjustments (1) to (4).   [5 *marks*]

(b) A revised revenue statement for the whole business for the year ended 30 September 1985.   [6 *marks*]

(AEB)

Answer 10.1

(a)

	Statford £	*Bington* £	*Andarstown* £
Profit/(loss) per statement	(17,000)	17,000	33,000
Manager's commission	0	800	1,000
Revised profit/(loss)	1,000	900	1,500
	(18,000)	15,300	30,500

(b)

Trading profit and loss for year ended 30 September 1985

	£	£
Sales		500,000
O/stock	44,000	
Purchases	300,000	
	344,000	
C/stock	51,600	
Cost of goods sold		292,400
Gross profit		207,600
Managers' commission	1,800	
Variable costs	75,000	
Fixed costs	55,000	
Other fixed costs	48,000	
		179,800
Net profit		27,800

93

11 Incomplete Records

11.1 Introduction

Questions on the topic of incomplete records present you with real-life situations where businesses are not keeping a full set of double entry records. The subject is also a favourite with examiners, since giving you the minimum of information and asking you to complete the accounts provides an excellent test of your understanding of accounting.

It is yet another topic that was introduced to you at 'O' level and is again examined frequently at 'A' level, but with increased complexity. You may need to refer to your 'O' level studies again but a reminder of the basic principles is given by way of summary below.

11.2 Statement of affairs

The statement of affairs is equivalent to the balance sheet where double entry records are kept. It lists assets and liabilities of a business in arriving at the net worth, which is equivalent to the owner's capital.

Where no other records are maintained, we can calculate the profit by comparing the net worth of the business at the start of a period with that at the end. The profit will be the increase in net worth, plus any drawings by the owner, less any capital introduced by him.

11.3 The trading and profit and loss account

In order to prepare the trading and profit and loss account, it is necessary to work from detailed cash and bank transactions. You should be prepared to reconstruct these from information given. You may have to insert opening or closing cash and/or bank balances as balancing figures. Alternatively, you may be given opening and closing balances but required to insert owner's drawings or expenses as a balancing figure.

Even if not required by the question, you are recommended as a first step in incomplete-record questions to start a workings page with the reconstructed cash and bank transactions. Once this is done, you can then start to calculate the other items as follows.

(i) *Sales* will be receipts from debtors and cash sales, plus closing debtors, less opening debtors. Also add back any discounts allowed.
(ii) *Purchases* will be payments to creditors and cash purchases, plus closing creditors, less opening creditors. Also add back any discounts received.

You may prefer to ascertain the figure by constructing a debtors and/or creditors control account. This would be equally acceptable.

In some questions you may not be given enough information to calculate sales and purchases by the above method. Instead you may be told the margin (gross profit as percentage of sales) or mark-up on purchase price. In this case calculate the figures which you are able to and insert the missing value as a balancing figure.

Example 11.2 illustrates the above technique: in this case we can calculate sales and, hence, gross profit. From this we arrive at the cost of goods sold, and add back closing stock, which gives us a figure representing opening stock plus purchases.

11.4 Worked examples

Example 11.1

Jim Turner, a manufacturer of wire baskets, keeps few accounting records and is able to provide only the following information for the financial year ended 30 September 1985.

	1 October 1984 £	30 September 1985 £
Cash	600	350
Bank overdraft	1,000	1,860
Creditors	2,300	2,600
Debtors	1,500	3,300
Rent prepaid	200	400
Plant and equipment: at cost less depreciation to date	5,000	?
Stocks at cost: raw materials	2,000	2,710
finished goods	4,000	3,260
J. Green	—	310

In addition the following information is available.
(1) J. Green, a regular customer, has paid £310 in advance for an order of baskets due to be delivered in November 1985.
(2) It is Turner's policy to depreciate the plant and equipment in his possession at the end of the financial year at the rate of 10 per cent of the book value. During the year ended 30 September 1985 Turner purchased a new item of plant at cost of £1,500. In addition a business associate has told Turner that a wire cutting machine similar to the one used in his business, which had a book value of £300, has recently been sold for £1,400.
(3) Included in the stock of raw materials on 30 September 1985 were some metal strips which cost £550 but which are unsuitable for use in production due to a modification in design. The metal strips have a scrap value of £120.
(4) Included in the stock of finished goods on 30 September 1985 were some specially designed baskets which had cost £590 to produce and which will be despatched to a customer during October invoiced at £950. In addition finished goods costing £400 which were delivered to a customer on a sale or return basis have been excluded from the closing stock figure.
(5) During the year, Turner had withdrawn £5,000 in cash from the business receipts. In April 1985 Turner accepted for his own use a supply of wire valued at £300 from a customer in full settlement of a debt of £400.

REQUIRED

(a) A detailed calculation of the profit of J. Turner for the year ended 30 September 1985. [17 marks]
(b) A statement of affairs of J. Turner as at 30 September 1985. [8 marks]
(AEB)

Solution 11.1

(a)
Calculation of capital balances:

	1 Oct. 1984		30 Sept. 1985	
	£	£	£	£
Cash		600		350
Debtors		1,500		3,300
Rent prepaid		200		400
Plant and equipment		5,000		5,850 [Note 1]
Stock of raw materials		2,000		2,280 [Note 2]
Stock of finished goods		4,000		3,660 [Note 3]
less:		13,300		15,840
J. Green			310	
Bank overdraft	1,000		1,860	
Creditors	2,300	3,300	2,600	4,770
Net worth [hence, capital]		10,000		11,070

NOTES

(1) Plant as at 1 October 1984	5,000
add Purchases	1,500
	6,500
less Depreciation at 10% of £6,500	650
	5,850

Note that realisable value is irrelevant for fixed assets.
(2) £2,710 less £430 reduction in value to realisable value.
(3) £3,260 plus £400 goods omitted.

J. Turner's profit is then

	£
Increase in net worth [£11,070 − £10,000]	1,070
add amounts withdrawn: cash	5,000
goods in settlement of debt	300
	6,370

(b)
Jim Turner: Statement of Affairs as at 30 September 1985

	£	£	£
Fixed assets			5,850
Current assets			
Stock		5,940	
Debtors and prepayments		3,700	
Cash		350	
		9,990	
less Current liabilities			
Creditors	2,600		
J. Green	310		
Bank overdraft	1,860	4,770	
Working capital			5,220
Net worth			11,070

Example 11.2

John Moss has been in business for several years, but has never bothered to keep a complete set of books. On 31 March 1983 he asked you to prepare a set of Final Accounts and a Balance Sheet, as he was thinking of expanding and needed to borrow some money. He thought that his chances would be easier if he could show 'something tangible'.

You find that Moss has not kept many records but was positive that his selling price was cost plus 20 per cent at all times. During the year he had paid £150,000 into the bank, most of which was his proceeds from sales. You also ascertain that at 31 March 1983, Moss has in stock goods for resale which cost him £5,000, which he says is about half what it was at the beginning of the year.

Moss owned his own premises which he valued at £100,000 and fittings which he said cost £80,000 when he bought them in April 1973, but he thought that now they were only worth £40,000. He also had an old van purchased in May 1978 for £2,500, which he was going to give away, as it was worthless.

From the counterfoils of Moss's cheque book you calculate that he has paid the following amounts during the year ending 31 March 1983:
  (i) Motor Van purchased on 30 March 1983 £7,250
 (ii) Rates for the year ending 30 June 1983 £750
(iii) Wages up to 24 March 1983 £3,060
 (iv) Lighting and Heating for the year £1,890
  (v) Sundry expenses £320
 (vi) Insurance for 18 months to 30 June 1983 £540
(vii) Personal cheques amounted to £10,400.

You can find no record of cheques sent to suppliers, and Moss explains that he uses a separate cheque book, which he has mislaid, but he has invoices outstanding of £2,450. By checking his Bank statements you calculate that he paid £118,810 to his creditors during the year and that he now has £9,930 in the bank.

Moss has only two credit customers and he has recorded that on 1 April they owed him £250 between them, they always paid in cash eventually, and at 31 March 1983 they owed him £155 each.

Moss won £5,000 at his bookmakers in September 1982, and as he had a few business debts outstanding he paid them from these winnings.

You find that Moss is in the habit of paying small expenses from his cash till; he can remember that at the end of last year he had £10 in the till and you check that at 31 March 1983 he has £90 in cash. Amongst the expenses he remembers paying are:

(a) The window cleaner who calls every week and is paid £5 for the shop windows and £2 for the windows of the house which Moss lives in.
(b) £10 for a donation to the British Legion in November, £5 to the RSPCA and £5 to various other charities.
(c) Wages to a lady who cleans the shop for £8 a week and to a lad who delivers for him for £5 a week.
(d) £5 a week for his own daily and Sunday papers.

Moss apologises for the mess his records are in but promises to pay you £50 when you have completed your work, with the promise to double it if he gets the loan.

Prepare suitable final accounts for the year ending 31 March 1983 as accurately as you can and a Balance Sheet at that date. Be careful to show all your working and to explain any assumptions that you make. [40]

(OLE)

Solution 11.2

Cash and bank account

		Cash £	Bank £			Cash £	Bank £
Apr. 1	Bal. b/d	10	2,950*	Mar. 31	Bank	150,000	
Mar. 31	Cash		150,000		Motor van		7,250
	Capital	5,000			Rates		750
	Sales				Wages [c]	676	3,060
	receipts	146,400*			Lighting and heating		1,890
					Sundry [a]	260	320
					Insurance		540
					Drawings [a + d]	364	10,400
					Creditors		118,810
					Donation	20	
					Bal. c/d	90	9,930
		151,410	152,950			151,410	152,950

*Balancing figures.

John Moss: Trading and Profit and Loss account for year ended 31 March 1983

	£	£
Sales [Note 1]		146,460
less Cost of sales		
Opening stock	10,000	
Purchases (5)	117,050	
(4)	127,050	
less Closing stock	5,000	
Cost of sales (3)		122,050
Gross profit (2)		24,410
Rates	750	
Wages	3,736	
Lighting and heating	1,890	
Sundry (£260 + £320 + £50)	630	
Insurance [£540 × $\frac{12}{18}$]	360	
Donations	20	
Depreciation – fittings [$\frac{1}{10}$ × £40,000]	4,000	
– motor van [$\frac{1}{5}$ × £2,500]	500	
		11,886
Net profit		12,524

NOTES

(1) Receipts from debtors £146,400; add debtors 31 March 1983 £310, less debtors 1 April 1982 £250.

(2) $\frac{20}{120} \times £146,460$.

(3) Sales 146,460, less gross profit 24,410.

(4) Cost of sales £122,050; add closing stock £5,000.

(5) From (4) above £127,050, less opening stock £10,000.

John Moss: Statement of Affairs at 1 April 1982

	£	£	£
Fixed assets			
Premises			100,000
Fittings [£40,000, add back $\frac{1}{10} \times £40,000$]			44,000
Motor van			500
			144,500
Current assets			
Stock		10,000	
Debtors		250	
Prepayments [Working 1]		187	
Bank		2,950	
Cash		10	
		13,397	
less Current liabilities			
Creditors [Working 2]	4,210		
Accrued expenses [Working 3]	90	4,300	
Working capital			9,097
Net worth			153,597

WORKING 1

Rates assuming unchanged $(\frac{3}{12} \times £750)$	187

WORKING 2

Payment to creditors — bank	118,810
Creditors at 31 March 1983	2,450
	121,260
Purchases (from trading account)	117,050
∴ Creditors at 1 April 1982	4,210

WORKING 3

Insurance $(\frac{3}{18} \times £540)$	90

	£	£
Fixed assets		
Premises		100,000
Fittings		40,000
Motor van		7,250
		147,250
Current assets		
Stock	5,000	
Debtors	310	
Prepayment [£187 + £90]	277	
Bank	9,930	
Cash	90	
	15,607	
less Current liabilities		
Creditors (£2,450 + £50)	2,500	
Working capital		13,107
		160,357
Capital		
Balance at 1 April 1982 [as opening Statement of Affairs]		153,597
add Capital introduced		5,000
add Net profit		12,524
		171,121
less Drawings		10,764
Balance at 31 March 1983		160,357

11.5   Further exercises

Question 11.1

S. Olsen, a wholesaler, did not keep proper books of account. The following information on his business was available on 31 March 1984:

	£		£
long-term loan	10,000	premises	50,000
motor vehicles	16,500	stock	12,500
trade debtors	23,650	trade creditors	14,500
balance at bank	10,500	cash in hand	3,400
fixtures and fittings	12,000	accrued general expenses	450

The balance at bank above included private investment income of his wife. This income arose from an interim dividend of 5 per cent and a final dividend of 11 per cent on 10,000 ordinary shares of 50p each.

The following information for the year ended 31 March 1985 was extracted from the cash book:

	Cash £	Bank £		Cash £	Bank £
Opening balances	3,400	10,500	Cash purchases		26,500
			Drawings		7,700
Receipts from trade		138,500	Payments to creditors		74,800
debtors (See Notes 2 and 3)			Salaries and wages	1,500	4,500
			Heating and lighting		1,500
			Motor vehicle expenses	180	4,020
			General expenses	270	2,230
			Receipts from trade		
			debtors banked	138,500	

Additional information:
(1) Discounts received during the year amounted to £1,100.
(2) Olsen calculates his selling price by adding 25 per cent profit on cost. All the goods sold in the year were sold at this mark-up except for £6,400 of the opening stock, which was marked up by $12\frac{1}{2}$ per cent only.
(3) All receipts from trade debtors were entered in the cash account, but the total amount received has not been recorded properly. The figure for bankings has been ascertained from bank statements.
(4) Depreciation to be provided:
   motor vehicles 20 per cent of book value
   fixtures and fittings 10 per cent of book value.
(5) £1,000 salaries and wages were owing at 31 March 1985.
(6) Interest at 11 per cent per annum on the long-term loan is to be provided for.
(7) Other balances at 31 March 1985 were:
   closing stock £15,700
   trade creditors £19,300
   trade debtors £11,000

REQUIRED

(a) A trading and profit and loss account for the year ended 31 March 1985. [*10 marks*]
(b) A balance sheet as at 31 March 1985. [*9 marks*]
(c) A concise statement giving **three** distinct advantages that a computerised accounting system could bring to Olsen's firm. [*6 marks*]

(AEB)

Answer 11.1

(a)

S. Olsen: Trading and Profit and Loss account for year ended 31 March 1985

	£	£
Sales		129,200 [Working 3]
Opening stock	12,500	
Purchases [Working 1]	107,200	
	119,700	
less Closing stock	15,700	
Cost of goods sold		104,000
Gross profit		25,200 [Working 2]
add Discounts received		1,100
		26,300
Salaries and wages [£6,000 + £1,000]	7,000	
Heating and lighting	1,500	
Motor vehicle expenses	4,200	
General expenses [£2,500 − £450]	2,050	
Depreciation — motor vehicles	3,300	
— fixtures and fittings	1,200	
Loan interest	1,100	20,350
Net profit		5,950

WORKING 1

Payments £74,800, add discounts received £1,100 plus creditors 31 March £19,300, less creditors 1 April £14,500 = £80,700, add cash purchases £26,500.

WORKING 2

	£
25% on (£104,000 − £6,400) =	24,400
$12\frac{1}{2}$% on £6,400 =	800
	25,200

Gross profit £25,200, add cost of goods sold £104,000.

S. Olsen: Statement of Affairs as at 1 April 1984

	£	£	£
Fixed assets			
Premises			50,000
Motor vehicles			16,500
Fixtures and Fittings			12,000
			78,500
Current assets			
Stock		12,500	
Debtors		23,650	
Bank		10,500	
Cash		3,400	
		50,050	
less Current liabilities			
Trade creditors	14,500		
Accrued expenses	450	14,950	
Working capital			35,100
			113,600
less Long-term loan			10,000
Net worth			103,600

(b)

S. Olsen Statement of Affairs as at 31 March 1985

	£	£	£
Fixed assets			
Premises			50,000
Motor vehicles [£16,500 − £3,300]			13,200
Fixtures and fittings [£12,000 − £1,200]			10,800
			74,000
Current assets			
Stock		15,700	
Debtors		11,000	
Bank [Note 1]		27,750	
Cash [Note 2]		4,800	
		59,250	
less Current liabilities			
Trade creditors	19,300		
Accrued wages and interest	2,100	21,400	37,850
			111,850
less Long-term loan			10,000
			101,850
Capital balance at 1 April 1984 (as above)*			103,600
add Net profit			5,950
			109,550
less Drawings			7,700
Balance at 31 March 1985			101,850

*Including wife's investment income £800.

NOTES

(1) Opening balance £10,500, add receipts £138,500, less payments £121,250.
(2) Sales £129,200, less debtors 31 March £11,000, add debtors 1 April £23,650 gives receipts from debtors £141,850. Receipts from debtors £141,850, add opening balance £3,400, less payments £140,450.

(c) Refer to Chapter 21.

Question 11.2

R. Gregg is a small wholesaler whose accounting year ends on 31 March each year. Because of staff shortages he was unable to complete his stocktaking on 31 March 1986 and this was not done until 6 April.

On that date the stock was valued at £102,450.

You offer to assist Gregg to calculate his stock as at 31 March and the following facts are found:

(a) A sale or return invoice from a supplier value £5,700 had been included in the stock sheets. No entry had been made in the accounting records for the delivery and none of the goods had been sold.
(b) Sales invoices during the period 31 March to 6 April amounted to £58,900; of this total, £3,840 covered goods despatched before 31 March. Gregg adds 25 per cent mark-up to cost.
(c) Suppliers' invoices received during the same period totalled £35,800; of this total, £1,580 covered goods received after 6 April.
(d) Stock sheet totals were incorrectly carried forward: on 31 December £102,403 was carried forward as £104,203 and on 28 February £83,200 was carried forward as £82,300.
(e) Returns to suppliers between 31 March and 6 April amounted to £1,820 and returns from customers at selling price were £4,740. Of the returns from customers, £1,380 had been marked up by 15 per cent. None of these returns had been entered on the stock sheets.

You are required to prepare a statement showing the value of stocks at 31 March 1986.

[18]
(OLE)

Answer 11.2

	£	£
Stock value as given at 6 April		102,450
less Goods on sale or return [a]	5,700	
Goods received 31 March to 6 April [c]	34,220	
Goods returned by customers 31 March to 6 April [e; Working 1]	3,888	43,808
		58,642
add Goods sent out 31 March to 6 April [b]		44,048
Returns to suppliers 31 March to 6 April [e]		1,820
Value of stocks at 31 March 1986		104,510

WORKING 1

$(£1,380 \times 100/115) + (£3,360 \times 125/100)$

Question 11.3

Len Jackson, a retailer who does not keep full accounting records, provided the following summarised bank account for the year ended 31 March 1984:

		£			£
1984			1983		
31 March	Cash receipts	86,020	1 April	Balance b/d	1,400
	Sale of fixed assets	1,500	1984		
	Sale of private motor car	5,000	31 March	Payments to trade	
				creditors	76,000
				Purchase of fixed assets	6,000
				Rates	2,000
				General expenses	4,500
				Balance c/d	2,620
		92,520			92,520

The following information is also available:

	31 March 1983	31 March 1984
	£	£
Premises	10,000	10,000
Stock	8,300	3,100
Trade creditors	1,610	3,610
Fixed assets	3,000	7,000
General expenses owing	130	350
Warehouse rent accrued	—	?

Before banking the receipts from cash sales Jackson withdrew £50 cash per week as drawings and paid wages of £120 per week. Although owning his own freehold shop, owing to lack of storage space Jackson rented a warehouse for £2,500 for the year. Unfortunately, the warehouse rented proved to be unsuitable and as a result Jackson had to discard some stock that was damaged by damp. The value of the stock discarded was not recorded and is not covered by insurance. However, Jackson has agreed with the owner of the warehouse that half of the stock loss can be deducted from the warehouse rent. A standard gross profit of 20 per cent on the cost of goods sold is earned.

REQUIRED

(a) A trading and profit and loss account for the year ended 31 March 1984.   [*11 marks*]
(b) The balance sheet as at 31 March 1984.   [*6 marks*]

(AEB)

Answer 11.3

Len Jackson: Trading and profit and loss account for the year ended 31 March 1984

	£	£
Sales [Note 1]		94,860
Opening stock	8,300	
Purchases [Note 2]	78,000	
	86,300	
less Closing stock	3,100	
Cost of goods sold		83,200
Gross profit		11,660
less Rates	2,000	
General expenses [Note 3]	4,720	
Wages	6,240	
Warehouse rent [Note 4]	425	
Depreciation [Note 5]	500	13,885
Net loss		2,225

NOTES

(1) £86,020 + £2,600 + £6,240.
(2) £76,000 + £3,610 − £1,610.
(3) £4,500 + £350 − £130.
(4) The gross profit expected on sales of £94,860 is £15,810. Since the gross profit is £11,660 (i.e. £4,150 less), the £4,150 is therefore the value of stock destroyed. Rent due is £2,500 less ($\frac{1}{2}$ × £4,150).
(5) Opening fixed assets £3,000, add purchases £6,000, less sales £1,500, gives £7,500. This compares with closing fixed assets £7,000 (i.e. a difference of £500).

(*continued opposite*)

Len Jackson: Balance Sheet as at 31 March 1984

	£	£
Fixed assets		
Premises		10,000
Other		7,000
		17,000
Current assets		
Stock	3,100	
Bank	2,620	
	5,720	
less Current liabilities		
Creditors [£3,610 + £425 + £350]	4,385	
Working Capital		1,335
Net Worth		18,335
Capital		
Balance as at 1 April 1983*		18,160
add Capital introduced (sale private car)		5,000
		23,160
less Net loss	2,225	
Drawings	2,600	4,825
Balance as at 31 March 1984		18,335

*Opening net worth £10,000 + £8,300 + £3,000 − £1,610 − £130 − £1,400.

12 Non-trading Organisations

12.1 Introduction

The topic of non-trading organisations is another of those introduced at 'O' level but frequently examined at 'A' level. The principles of accounting for these organisations, as covered by the 'O' level, do not change; however, the worked examples and further exercises will show you the type of question that you should be prepared to tackle.

By their very nature, such organisations will seldom keep full double entry records. For this reason you will bring into use many of the techniques demonstrated in Chapter 11.

12.2 Receipts and payments account

As the name suggests, the receipts and payments account is a record of cash and bank receipts and payments which have actually occurred. It commences with the cash and bank balances at the beginning of the period, adds receipts, deducts payments, and ends with the cash and bank balances at the period end.

12.3 Income and expenditure account

A receipts and payments account only provides us with information on the increase or decrease in bank balances. It does not show us a true surplus or deficit for the year: in order to do this, we must follow the accruals or matching concept described in Chapter 1. That is to say, we should look at the actual income and expenditures relevant to the accounting period. For example, we want to include subscriptions due but not received, and expenses incurred but not paid for. Conversely, we need to exclude subscriptions prepaid in respect of next year and prepayments made in respect of expenses.

The income and expenditure account takes the amounts from the receipts and payment account and adjusts them for accruals and prepayments as given above. It thus gives us a fair picture of the surplus or deficit for the year.

12.4 Accumulated fund

The accumulated fund can be looked upon as equivalent to the capital account in respect of trading organisations. The balance on the income and expenditure account is transferred to this accumulated fund.

12.5 Other funds

Apart from the general or accumulated fund, many organisations have other funds for specific purposes. Often these will be represented by specific investments or held in separate accounts. As far as the balance sheet is concerned, these will appear as an asset, while the fund will appear as a liability. Where the fund has income during the year, this will not appear in the income and expenditure account; however, the fund in the balance sheet will increase, as will the investments or bank account representing that fund.

12.6 Worked examples

Example 12.1

The Av One wine society exists for two reasons, to promote the drinking of good wines and to enable members to obtain wines at a reasonable price.

A monthly magazine is issued and sold to the public; members of the society are able to obtain a copy at half price. During the year ending 31 May 1984 the following transactions were recorded by the society treasurer:

1. The society has 325 registered members and the annual subscription of £25 per member was received from 304 of them; of these, ten members also paid their subscription to 31 May 1985. Four members (not included above) owed subscriptions for the year to 31 May 1983 and they paid £200 during the year. Of the remaining membership, three had paid two years' subscription during the year ending 31 May 1983.
2. 5,000 copies of the magazine had been sold at 75p per copy. None of the members had taken advantage of the half price offer.
3. The cost of printing the magazine was £5,240, but advertising revenue from local wine retailers was £1,480. At the end of the year 100 copies of the magazine had not been sold; it was the usual practice to offer these at wine tastings during the following year at 40p per copy. It is anticipated that they will all be sold. Copies of the magazine in stock at 31 May 1983 were valued at £30. These had all been sold at the first wine tasting in September 1983.
4. A fund had been set up from donations received to enable a connoisseurs' wine tasting session to be held each year. At 31 May 1983 the fund stood at £525 and during the year further donations to this fund had been received and banked totalling £150, and £15 interest on the special account at the bank had been credited. The expenses of the wine tasting session held during the year, excluding the cost of the wine, were £300. The cost of the wine was covered entirely by the members who had attended the function.
5. The society had no premises of their own but were able to hold meetings and functions at the local golf club. The rent for the year was £2,500. The society held stocks of wine for resale on the premises and at 31 May 1983 these were valued at £3,220.
6. Payments for wine during the year, purchased for resale, were £182,000 and at 31 May 1984 £2,400 remained unsold. Receipts from sales of wine were £186,000. Payments for wine for ordinary wine tasting sessions held during the year were £8,215; there was none in stock at 31 May 1984.
7. Apart from the information that can be obtained from above, the treasurer has kept the following records:
    (i) At 31 May 1983, cash in hand was £42 and the ordinary current account at the bank had a balance of £3,460. The cash in hand at 31 May 1984 was £42.
    (ii) Ordinary expenses of running the society paid out of bank were: postage etc. £400, insurance £550, gratuities to golf club staff £150, hire of glasses etc. £1,250, advertising £260.
    (iii) Sundry expenses had been paid out of cash and during the year £140 had been withdrawn from the bank and held by the treasurer to pay them.

(iv) Creditors for wine purchased for resale were £1,200 at 31 May 1983 and £1,350 at 31 May 1984.

(v) At 31 May 1983 members of the society owed £420 for wines purchased and £530 was owing by members at 31 May 1984.

You are required to prepare:

(a) A Recipts and Payments Account and Revenue (Income and Expenditure) Account for the year ending 31 May 1984 and

(b) A Balance Sheet of the Society at 31 May 1984. [40]

(OLE)

Solution 12.1

(a)

Av One wine society: Receipts and payments account for year ended 31 May 1984

		£			£
Receipts			Payments		
June 1	Balance b/d [Note 1]	4,027	May 31 Magazine printing		5,240
May 31	Subscription [Note 2]	8,050	Expenses		300
	Magazine sales [Note 3]	3,780	Rent		2,500
	Magazine advertising	1,480	Wine purchases (resale)		182,000
	Donations	150	Wine purchases (tasting)		8,215
	Interest	15	Postage		400
	Wine sales	186,000	Insurance		550
	Wine sales (tasting)	8,215	Gratuities		150
			Hire of glasses		1,250
			Advertising		260
			Sundry		140
			Balance c/d [Note 4]		10,712
		211,717			211,717

NOTES

(1) £3,460 (general) + £42 (cash) + £525 (connoisseurs' fund).
(2) (£25 × 304) + (25 × 10) + £200.
(3) (5000 × 75p) + [from paragraph 3] £30.
(4) Balancing figure. Cash is £42 and connoisseurs' fund £690; therefore general account is £9,980.

A subscription account, while not required, will help explain the figures in the Income and expenditure account and Balance Sheet.

Subscriptions

		£			£
June 1	Balance b/d (4)	100	June 1 Balance b/d (3)		75
	Income and expenditure (325)	8,125	May 31 Receipts		8,050
May 31	Balance c/d (10)	250	May 31 Balance c/d (14)		350
		8,475			8,475

The 14 debtors at May 31 1984 is calculated from the information given (325 − 304 − 4 − 3).

Av One wine society: Income and expenditure account for year ended 31 May 1984

		£
Income		
Subscriptions		8,125
Magazine profit [Working 1]		30
Profit on wine sales [Working 2]		3,140
		11,295
less Expenditure		
Expenses re wine tasting sessions	300	
Rent of premises	2,500	
Postage	400	
Insurance	550	
Gratuities	150	
Hire of glasses	1,250	
Advertising	260	
Sundry	140	5,550
Surplus for year		5,745

WORKING 1

	£	£
Sales revenue		3,780
Advertising revenue		1,480
		5,260
Magazine printing costs	5,240	
less Increase in stocks [£40 − £30]	10	5,230
Magazine profit		30

(b)

Av One wine society: Balance Sheet as at 31 May 1983

	£	£
Current assets		
Stock of magazines		30
Stock of wines		3,220
Subscriptions due		100
Debtors for wines		420
Bank (general)		3,460
Bank (connoisseurs' session fund)		525
Cash		42
		7,797
less Current liabilities		
Subscriptions in advance	75	
Creditors for wine	1,200	1,275
		6,522
Represented by		
Connoisseur's wine tasting fund		525
General fund (balancing figure)		5,997
		6,522

Av One wine society: Balance Sheet as at 31 May 1984

	£	£
Current assets		
Stock of magazines		40
Stock of wines		2,400
Subscriptions due		350
Debtors for wines		530
Bank (general)		9,980
Bank (connoisseur's session fund)		690
Cash		42
		14,032
less Current liabilities		
Subscriptions in advance	250	
Creditors for wine	1,350	1,600
		12,432
Represented by		
Connoisseurs' wine tasting fund		690
General fund [£5,997 + £5,745]		11,742
		12,432

		£	£
(2)	Wine sales [£186,000 + £530 − £420]		186,110
	Opening stock	3,220	
	Purchases [£182,000 + £1,350 − £1,200	182,150	
		185,370	
	less Closing stock	2,400	
			182,970
	Profit		3,140

Example 12.2

The Greenfields Tennis Club has been established for many years but recently its financial position has declined. The treasurer of the club has prepared the following receipts and payments account for the year ended 30 September 1984.

1983		£	1984		£
1 October	Balance b/d	6,740	30 September	Affiliation to County Tennis Association	250
1984				Purchase of tennis balls	180
30 September	Sales of tennis balls	260		Dance expenses	650
	Dance receipts	390		Wages	2,400
	Sale of fixtures	180		General expenses	2,680
	Subscriptions	4,310		Balance c/d	5,720
		11,880			11,880
1984					
1 October	Balance b/d	5,720			

The following information is also available.

	30 September 1983 £	30 September 1984 £
Pavilion	6,000	6,000
Stock of tennis balls	30	20
Fixtures and equipment	2,400	2,000
Subscriptions in advance	40	60
General expenses owing	70	110

The club has received planning permission to build four squash courts at a total cost of £120,000, and is considering two offers to finance the development.

Swiftshoe Ltd, a sports shoe manufacturer with a large local factory, has offered an interest free loan of £120,000 over five years in return for free membership for fifty of its employees and the exclusive use of the facilities for two weeks per annum without charge to host the Swiftshoe National Squash Championships, an event that regularly attracts 500 spectators per day from throughout the United Kingdom. In addition the firm requires the club to change its name to The Swiftshoe Squash and Tennis Club.

The local council has also offered an interest free loan of £120,000 over five years but insists that membership subscriptions be limited to £25 per annum. If agreement between the club and the council is not reached, the council intends to build another squash complex half a mile from the Greenfields club.

The club has been advised that 600 members is the maximum number for four squash courts and that a separate membership subscription of £50 could be charged to squash members. At present there is no squash club in the area and it is anticipated that the club would be fully subscribed. It is expected that £300 per week would be received in court fees and that the annual running costs of the courts would be £5,000.

REQUIRED

(a) The income and expenditure account for the year ended 30 September 1984 of the Greenfields Tennis Club. [7 marks]
(b) A balance sheet as at 30 September 1984 of the Greenfields Tennis Club. [4 marks]
(c) Consider the alternatives open to the club concerning the proposed squash court development. [14 marks]

(AEB)

Solution 12.2

(a)

Greenfields Tennis Club: Income and expenditure account for year ended 30 September 1984

	£	£
Income		
Subscriptions [Note 1]		4,290
Profit on sale of tennis balls [Note 2]		70
		4,360
less Expenditures		
Loss on dances [£650 − £390]	260	
Depreciation of fixtures [Note 3]	220	
Affiliation to County Tennis Association	250	
Wages	2,400	
General expenses [Note 4]	2,720	5,850
Deficit for year		(1,490)

NOTES

(1) £4,310 + £40 − £60.
(2) Cost of balls sold is £180 + £30 − £20 = £190. Profit, therefore, is £70 (£260 − £190).
(3) Fixtures are worth £400 less (£4,400 − £4,000); however, £180 received from sale of fixtures.
(4) £2,680 + £110 − £70.

(b)

Greenfields Tennis Club: Balance Sheet as at 30 September 1984

	£	£	£
Fixed assets			
Pavilion			6,000
Fixtures			2,000
			8,000
Current assets			
Stock of tennis balls		20	
Bank		5,720	
		5,740	
less Current liabilities			
Accrued expenses	110		
Subscriptions in advance	60	170	
Working capital			5,570
Net assets			13,570
Represented by			
Accumulated fund balance at 1 October*			15,060
less Deficit for year			1,490
			13,570

*£6,740 + £6,000 + £30 + £2,400 + £40 − £70 = £15,060.

(c)
The financial effects can be summarised as follows:

Swiftshoe	£
Membership fees [550 × £50]	27,500
Court fees [50 weeks at (550/600) × £300]	13,750
	41,250
less Running costs	5,000
Surplus	36,250

Council	£
Membership fees [600 × £25]	15,000
Court fees [52 weeks at £300]	15,600
	30,600
less Running costs	5,000
Surplus	25,600

The Swiftshoe offer would appear to be the better financially. However, additional considerations are:

(i) Would the club be fully subscribed when the council builds an alternative complex?

(ii) Would the non-Swiftshoe members accept the closure of the club to them for two weeks?

(iii) Would the tennis members accept the change of name?

(iv) Could additional income be earned from the 500 spectators attending the championships?

12.7 Further exercises

Question 12.1

The following receipts and payments account for the year ended 31 May 1983 has been prepared by the treasurer of the Smilers Social Club.

		£				£
1982			1983			
1 June	Balance b/d	3,100	31 May	Bar purchases		6,200
				Dance expenses		1,870
1983				Rates		1,360
31 May	Subscriptions	6,310		Wages		3,000
	Bar receipts	9,720		General expenses		3,790
	Dance receipts	3,100		Purchase of fixtures		1,500
	Sale of fixtures	100		Balance c/d		4,610
		22,330				22,330

		£
1983		
1 June	Balance b/d	4,610

The following information is also available:

	31 May 1982	31 May 1983
Subscriptions in advance	40	120
Bar stock	3,980	1,210
Bar purchases owing	470	360
General expenses owing	70	45
Fixtures (at cost less depreciation)	10,000	11,000
Premises	12,000	12,000
Rates pre-paid	410	590

The treasurer of the club is concerned at the reduction in the size of the bar stock. Upon investigation it has been discovered that bar stock with a resale value of £900 has been delivered, on a sale or return basis, to a club member for a private function and that this transaction has not been entered anywhere in the accounts. An overall profit margin of 30 per cent on sales is earned by bar sales.

REQUIRED

(a) The club's income and expenditure account for the year ended 31 May 1983 showing clearly the profit on bar sales. *[14 marks]*

(b) A balance sheet as at 31 May 1983. *[7 marks]*

(c) A computation of the bar stock deficiency at 31 May 1983. *[5 marks]*

(AEB)

Answer 12.1

(a)

Smiler's Social Club: Bar trading account for year ended 31 May 1983

	£	£
Sales		9,720
Opening stock	3,980	
Purchases [£6,200 + £360 − £470]	6,090	
	10,070	
less Closing stock*	1,840	8,230
Bar profit		1,490

*£1,210 plus 70% × £900.

Smiler's Social Club: Income and expenditure account for year ended 31 May 1983

	£	£
Income		
Subscriptions [£6,310 + £40 − £120]		6,230
Bar profit		1,490
Dance profit [£3,100 − £1,870]		1,230
		8,950
Expenditures	£	£
Rates [£1,360 + £410 − £590]	1,180	
Wages	3,000	
General expenses [£3,790 − £70 + £45]	3,765	
Depreciation fixtures [Note 1]	400	8,345
Surplus for year		605

NOTE 1

Opening figure is £10,000; add purchases £1,500, less sales £100, gives £11,400. Year-end figure is £11,000; therefore, depreciation is £400 (£11,400 − £11,000).

(b)

Smiler's Social Club: Balance Sheet as at 31 May 1983

	£	£	£
Fixed assets			
Premises			12,000
Fixtures			11,000
			23,000
Current assets			
Bar stock		1,840	
Rates prepaid		590	
Bank		4,610	
		7,040	
less Current liabilities			
Creditors	360		
Accrued expenses	45		
Subscriptions prepaid	120	525	6,515
Net assets			29,515
Represented by			
Accumulated fund balance at 1 June 1982*			28,910
add Surplus for year			605
			29,515

*£3,100 − £40 + £3,980 − £470 − £70 + £10,000 + £12,000 + £410.

	£
(c) Bar profit expected is 30% × £9,720 =	2,916
Actual bar profit	1,490
Bar stock deficiency	1,426

Question 12.2

Explain the differences between a Receipts and Payments Account and an Income and Expenditure Account. When would one be used in preference to the other?

Answer 12.2

Refer to the text. The former reflects actual cash incomings and outgoings; the latter reflects actual income, expenditure appropriate to that period. The latter is usually more meaningful.

Question 12.3

(a) The treasurer of the Sprightly Sports Club gives you the following information:

At 31 March 1985 the club has premises which cost £62,000 and equipment valued at £40,000. Bar stocks are worth £4,500, while £250 is owing to suppliers. Members with accounts at the bar owe £1,200. Subscriptions totalling £200 have been paid up to 31 March 1986, but £50 is owing for the year ending 31 March 1985.

The club has established a trust from various legacies for use as prizes in annual sports competitions; at 31 March 1985 investment of these legacies are £4,000 in a Building Society and £2,000 in an Investment Trust. At the same date the club has a life-members fund of £500.

You are required to calculate the accumulated fund of the club at 31 March 1985.

(b) The following information is made available by Charles Wilde:

	31 May 1984 £	31 May 1985 £
Debtors	20,000	25,200
Creditors	15,000	14,100
Stock	4,000	3,000

During the year ending 31 May 1985, £65,000 has been paid into the bank from debtors and cash sales. £42,000 has been paid to creditors. Discounts allowed by Wilde amount to £2,400 and those allowed by his creditors were £3,900.

Before paying his takings into the bank Wilde has paid wages of £100 per week and expenses of £4,200 per annum.

You are required to calculate the Net Profit of Wilde for the year ending 31 May 1985. [18 marks]

(OLE)

Answer 12.3

(a)

	£	£
Assets: Premises £62,000 + Equipment £40,000 + Stocks £4,500 + Bar accounts £1,200 + Subscriptions in arrears £50		107,750
less Liabilities: Suppliers £250 + Subscriptions prepaid £200		450
Accumulated fund		107,300

The investments in the building society and the investment trust are equal to the amount of the trust fund and are therefore ignored in the above calculation.

(b)

	£	£
Sales [Working 1]		82,000
Opening stock	4,000	
Purchases [Working 2]	45,000	
	49,000	
less Closing stock	3,000	46,000
Gross profit		36,000
add Discounts received		3,900
		39,900
less Discounts allowed	2,400	
Wages	5,200	
Expenses	4,200	11,800
Net profit		28,100

WORKING 1

£65,000 + £5,200 (wages) + £4,200 (expenses) + £2,400 (discounts) + £25,200 (closing debtors) − £20,000 (opening debtors).

£42,000 + £3,900 (discounts) + £14,100 (closing creditors) − £15,000 (opening creditors).

Question 12.4

(a) John Bull gets his computer to give him an Aged Debtors list at the end of each month from which he decides which debts he can write off as bad. He also keeps a provision for Doubtful Debts account of 4 per cent of his debtors at the year end. In his accounts for the year ending 31 May 1982 he increased his doubtful debts provision to £780.

At 31 May 1983 he has written off £1,240 as bad debts. His debtors at the same date are £18,400. His total sales for the year to 31 May 1983 were £400,000, of which 50 per cent were for cash; he has allowed £2,700 in cash discounts and returns from credit customers were £6,240.

Prepare the Debtors Control account for the year ending 31 May 1983 in John Bull's books.

(b) The High Flyers Senior Citizens Club has 160 members. The following information is available for the year ending 31 December 1982. The Annual Subscription is £2. Forty of the members had paid two years' subscriptions on 1 January 1982 and at 31 December 1982 ten members still owe their subscriptions.

Thirty of the members joined the club after 1 June 1982 and were only charged £1 for the remainder of the year, but four of these paid £3 to cover them to 31 December 1983.

You are required to calculate:

 (i) The total subscriptions received during the year.

(ii) The total subscriptions to be included in the Revenue Account for the year ending 31 December 1982. [*18 marks*]

(OLE)

Answer 12.4

(a)

Debtors control

		£			£
June 1	Balance b/d [Note 1]	19,500	May 31	Discounts allowed	2,700
May 31	Sales	200,000		Sales returns	6,240
				Bad debts	1,240
				Bank [Note 2]	190,920
				balance c/d	18,400
		219,500			219,500

NOTES

(1) (100/4) × £780.
(2) Balancing figure.

(b)

		£
(i)	30 new members at £1	30
	4 new members an additional £2	8
	(160 − 30 − 40 − 10) × £2	160
	Received during year	198
(ii)	130 at £2	260
	30 at £1	30
		290

	£
Alternatively,	
Subscriptions prepaid at beginning of year [40 × £2]	80
Subscriptions received during year [as above]	198
Subscriptions in arrears at end of year [10 × £2]	20
	298
less Subscriptions prepaid at end of year [4 × £2]	8
	290

13 Valuation of Stock

13.1 Introduction

Valuation of stock is subjective. However, there are some established 'methods' and principles which are commonly applied. The physical units or quantities of stock may be valued in several alternative ways, depending on the method applied. This will obviously affect trading profits, in as much as various possible values of opening and closing stock will affect the trading and net profits for each period under review.

13.1 FIFO, LIFO, AVCO

The *FIFO* (First In First Out) method assumes that stock is issued or sold in the order in which it was purchased or made – i.e. the oldest stock is issued or sold first.

The *LIFO* (Last In First Out) method assumes that stock is issued or sold in the order of the most recent purchase or units produced – i.e. the newest stock is issued or sold first.

The *AVCO* (Average Cost) method places an average value on each unit of stock (a weighted average) and simply multiplies this average by the number of units remaining in stock, to arrive at a total stock value.

13.3 Perpetual vs. periodic

Depending on the sophistication of the firm's information and stock control system, a valuation of stocks can be revised after every transaction which involves the movement of stock (perpetual valuation), or a valuation of stock can be made just at the end of each trading period (periodic valuation).

A firm may value its stock by the FIFO, LIFO or AVCO method; it may conduct this valuation either 'perpetually' or 'periodically'.

We can illustrate by applying each of these alternatives to the same data.

	Purchases	Sales
Month 1	400 units at £20 each	300 units at £35 each
Month 2	600 units at £22 each	550 units at £35 each
Month 3	500 units at £23 each	450 units at £35 each

Let us assume that the firm values stock using FIFO, on a perpetual basis. At the end of each month its stock values will be as follows:

end of month 1 – $(400 - 300) \times £20 = £2,000$
end of month 2 – $(100 + 600 - 550) \times £22 = £3,300$
[The firm assumes that the stock remaining is the newest stock.]
end of month 3 – $(150 + 500 - 450) \times £23 = £4,600$

On a perpetual LIFO basis, the firm would arrive at the following valuations:

end of month 1 − (400 − 300) × £20   = £2,000
end of month 2 − (100 + 600 − 550) × £20 = £3,000
end of month 3 − (150 + 500 − 450) = 200 units, split as follows:
   150 at £20 = £3,000
    50 at £22 = £1,100
           = £4,100

All of the stock purchases in month 3 are assumed to have been sold in month 3 (Last In First Out).

On a perpetual AVCO basis, the firm would arrive at the following valuation:

end of month 1 − (400 − 300) units at an average cost of £20 = £2,000.
   During month 2 the firm had
     100 at £20 = £2,000

and

   600 at £22 = £13,200
   700   £15,200

The average cost of these units was £15,200/700 = £21.71. It has 150 units in stock at the end of month 2. Therefore, the value of closing stock at the end of month 2 is 150 × £21.71 = £3,256.50.
During month 3, the firm had
    150 at £21.71 = £ 3,256.50

and

   500 at £23   = £11,500.00
   650   £14,756.50

The average cost of these units was £14,756.50/650 = £22.70. It has 200 units in stock at the end of month 3. Its value will be 200 × £22.70 = £4,540.

We can now examine the periodic valuations.

Periodic FIFO   During three months the firm purchased 1,500 units and sold 1,300 units, leaving a closing stock of 200 units; these are assumed to be the newest units − i.e. 200 at £23 = £4,600.

Periodic LIFO   Assume a closing stock of 200 of the oldest stock − i.e. 200 at £20 = £4,000.

Periodic AVCO needs a little more calculation. We must calculate the weighted average cost of the stock we had available for sale over the whole period. The firm purchased 1,500 units for a total cost of £32,810. The average cost of these was £32,810/1,500 = £21.87. At the end of month 3, there are 200 units in stock. Their value is 200 × £21.87 = £4,374.

Note that in both periodic and perpetual stock valuation the AVCO valuation falls between (but not necessarily exactly in the middle of) the FIFO and LIFO valuations.

13.4 Inflation

If production costs and/or unit purchasing costs are constant, our valuation of stock would be the same under any of the three methods described above. It is only because costs are changing that our valuation of closing stock can vary, depending on the system of valuation used.

It is important to remember a simple rule about changing costs and stock valuation. It is: In periods of rising costs (inflation), the FIFO system will result in a higher value of closing stock than LIFO. This is because the firm is left with the more expensive units of stock, having sold the oldest (and therefore the cheaper) units first.

13.5 Effects on trading profits

There is no hard and fast rule to apply here, apart from remembering the connection between opening and closing stock, costs of goods sold and gross profit – i.e. a simple trading account:

	£	£
Sales		xxx
O/stock	xxx	
add Purchases	xxx	
	xxx	
less Closing stock	xxx	
Cost of goods sold		xxx
Gross profit		xxx

We can see that the higher the value of opening stock the higher will be the cost of goods sold, and thus the lower will be gross profit. The higher the value of closing stock, the higher the value of gross profit.

In a firm's first year of trade, under conditions of rising costs, FIFO will yield higher closing stock values and therefore larger gross profit.

But, remember that the *closing* stock of one period becomes the *opening* stock of the next, thus pushing down the gross profit of the second period.

13.6 Cost and net realisable value

An important accounting principle is that of 'conservatism', as regards the valuation of assets or measurement of profit.

Having valued stocks by any one of the methods described above (FIFO, LIFO, AVCO), the firm should compare the result with the net realisable value of the stock – i.e. how much the stock could be sold for, after taking into account any additional costs it would incur to put the stock into a marketable condition. The stock should then be valued at the lower of cost or net realisable value.

Example Using traditional FIFO methods of stock valuation, the closing stock is valued at £5,000, but the maximum price the stock could be sold for is £2,000, and this could only be realised if £200 was spent modifying the stock. The net realisable value is therefore £1,800. The stock should be valued now at The lower of cost (£5,000) and net realisable value (£1,800) – i.e. £1,800.

13.7 Worked examples

Example 13.1

During the first six months of 1986, a firm has the following pattern of receipts and issues of a particular raw material.

Receipts		Issues	
10 Jan	15 items @ £25	16 Feb	18 items
28 Feb	20 items @ £26	23 Mar	11 items
17 May	13 items @ £26.80	27 June	14 items

(a) Using the Average Cost (AVCO) method, show the value of closing stock after each stock movement. Stock on hand at 1 January 1986 comprised 12 items with a total value of £240.

(b) Use your figures to evaluate the AVCO approach as a method of valuing materials issues.

Solution 13.1

[Look at the dates carefully.]

(a)

	Receipts	Issues	Units in c/stock	AVCO per unit	Value of c/stock
O/stock	12	–	12	£20	£240
10 Jan.	15	–	12+15 = 27	£615/27 = £22.78	240+(15 × 25) £615
16 Feb.	–	18	27−18=9	£22.78	9 × 22.78 = £205.02
28 Feb.	20	–	29	725.02/29 = £25.00	£205.02+(20 × 26) £725.02
23 Mar.	–	11	18	£25.00	18 × £25 = £450
17 May	13	–	31	798.40/31 = £25.75	£450+(13 × 26.80) = £798.40
27 June	–	14	17	£25.75	17 × £25.75 = £437.75

[Notice that the per unit value only changes when stock is received, not when stock is issued (or sold).]

(b) Applying AVCO to raw materials, particularly on a perpetual basis, produces a constantly changing cost per unit of raw material used. If the firm is not using a standard costing system, its cost of production will also be changing every time new raw materials are received. This yields an uncertainty for the firm in terms of finished goods costs and selling prices, etc.

The system used required several instances of figures being rounded off, where perhaps this degree of accuracy is unnecessary in a raw material turnover of such small quantities.

Example 13.2

The Reliable Cash and Carry Wholesalers Limited sell a range of household durable goods at a uniform gross profit of 25 per cent above cost. Occasionally goods are damaged in the storerooms or soiled after display use and have to be offered at a lower than normal selling price. The following figures in the company's books refer to the year ended 31 March 1983:

	£
Stock at 1 April 1982	10,080
Sales	209,853
Purchases	176,820

The stock at 1 April 1982 was subsequently sold for £12,306 and is included in the sales figure of £209,853.

Included in the purchases figure of £176,820 are goods which cost £36,120 but which are marked down to a selling price of £42,504. These 'reduced' goods were sold during the year with the exception of goods remaining in stock, which cost £420 and had been marked down to £357.

REQUIRED

(a) Calculate the value of the stock at 31 March 1983 at cost price.
(b) (i) Explain the principle inherent in the 'lower of cost or net realisable value' rule.
    (ii) Trading account for the year ended 31 March 1983.

(L)

Solution 13.2

(a) This is really a question involving the tracking of stock movements. We must calculate the cost of goods sold by calculating which sales were made at the normal margin.

	Sale price	Cost price
	£	£
Total sales	209,853	
Less sales of opening stock	12,306	10,080
sales of marked down goods		
[£42,504 − £357] =	42,147	35,700
Sales at normal margin	155,400	124,320
Cost price of goods sold at normal margin		170,100
= (100/125) × £155,400 =		

Thus, value of closing stock at cost =

	£
O/stock at cost	10,080
add Purchases at cost	176,820
	186,900
less Cost of goods sold	170,100
Closing stock at cost	16,800

As some closing stock has a net realisable value of £357, as opposed to a cost price of £420, we must choose the net realisable value. Therefore, closing stock is now £16,800 − (£420 − £357) = £16,737.

(b) (i) See Section 13.6.

(ii)   Trading account year ended 31 March 1973

	£	£
Sales		209,853
O/stock	10,080	
Purchases	176,820	
	186,900	
C/stock	16,737	
Cost of goods sold		170,163
Gross profit		39,690

Example 13.3

The Big Box Manufacturing Co. Ltd, which buys raw materials and some finished goods, has been using the LIFO method of stock control for some years, and is now considering changing to the FIFO method. To consider the effects on profits, it is decided that the accounts for the six months to 31 March 1982 should be prepared using both methods for valuing stock. The following information for the six months ending 31 March (LIFO) is available:

<table>
<tr><td></td><td></td><td>£</td></tr>
<tr><td>1. Costs:</td><td>Raw Materials consumed</td><td>210,000</td></tr>
<tr><td></td><td>Direct labour</td><td>150,000</td></tr>
<tr><td></td><td>Indirect costs</td><td>120,000</td></tr>
<tr><td></td><td>Selling and distribution</td><td>80,000</td></tr>
<tr><td></td><td>Administration</td><td>40,000</td></tr>
<tr><td></td><td>Finance</td><td>10,000</td></tr>
</table>

<table>
<tr><td>2. Stocks:</td><td></td><td>1 Oct. 81</td><td>31 Mar. 82</td></tr>
<tr><td></td><td>Work in progress</td><td>£3,000</td><td>£7,000</td></tr>
<tr><td></td><td>Raw materials</td><td>12,500 tons</td><td>?</td></tr>
<tr><td></td><td>Finished goods</td><td>3,500 units</td><td>?</td></tr>
</table>

3. Cost of stocks at 1 October 1981:
   Raw materials   80 pence per ton
   Finished goods   £2 per unit

4. Purchases for the year:

October	50,000 tons at £1 ton	20,000 units at £2.50 each
December	60,000 tons at £1.50 ton	10,000 units at £2.70 each
January	30,000 tons at £1.80 ton	5,000 units at £3 each
March	10,000 tons at £2 ton	

5. All the goods manufactured in any month are sold by the end of that month.
6. The method of valuing stock of work in progress is not to be changed.
7. Sales for the six months were £880,000, which under present stock methods gives a mark-up of 60 per cent on the cost of goods sold.
8. Each half-year a bonus is distributed to the employees of $33\frac{1}{3}$ per cent of the Net Profit; it has been agreed that the amount to be distributed should never be less than £70,000.
9. Each year £40,000 is transferred to reserves and 50 per cent of the remaining profits are retained in the business.

Prepare the accounts for the six months ending 31 March 1982, showing as much information as possible, using both methods of valuing stock, and show how much profit would be available for dividends to shareholders under each method.

(OLE)

Solution 13.3

We must produce manufacturing, trading profit and loss a/c for six months, using FIFO and LIFO.

Let us look at LIFO. There is a missing figure for closing stock of raw materials. From the information in the question we are told:

		£
Opening stock 12,500 tons @ 80p per ton =		10,000
Purchases	50,000 tons @ £1	50,000
	60,000 tons @ £1.50	90.000
	30,000 tons @ £1.80	54,000
	10,000 tons @ £2.00	20,000
Total		224,000
less Raw material consumed (note 1 of question)		210,000
Therefore Closing stock of raw material		14,000

This has been valued on LIFO, and must be represented by

	£10,000 worth of 80p per ton i.e.	12,500 tons
and	£4,000 worth of £1 per ton i.e.	4,000 tons
Total		16,500 tons

Under FIFO, these 16,500 tons would be valued as

		£
	10,000 at £2 per ton =	20,000
and	6,500 at £1.80 per ton =	11,700
Total		31,700

There is also a missing figure for closing stock of finished goods. We know that sales were £880,000 with a mark-up (under LIFO) of 60 per cent. Therefore, the cost of Sales = £880,000 × (100/160) = £550,000 (LIFO).

Big Box Manufacturing Co. Ltd: LIFO Manufacturing, trading, profit and loss account 6 months ended 31 March 1982

	£	£
Sales		880,000
O/stock raw materials	10,000	
Purchases	214,000	
	224,000	
C/stock raw materials	14,000	
Raw materials consumed	210,000	
Direct labour	150,000	
Prime cost	360,000	
Indirect costs	120,000	
Total factory cost	480,000	
add O/stock work in progress	3,000	
	483,000	
deduct C/stock work in progress	7,000	
cost of completed goods	476,000	
add O/stock of finished goods [3,500 units @ £2]	7,000	
Purchases of finished goods [20 × 2.50, + 10 × 2.7 + 5 × 3]	92,000	
	575,000	
Closing stock of finished goods [by deduction]	25,000	
Cost of goods sold [see above working]		550,000
Gross profit		330,000
less Selling and distribution	80,000	
Administration	40,000	
Finance	10,000	130,000
Net profit before bonus		200,000
Bonus		70,000
Net profit		130,000
Transfer to reserves	20,000	
Dividends [50% of (130,000 − 20,000)]	55,000	75,000
Retained profits		55,000

Big Box Manufacturing Co. Ltd: FIFO Manufacturing, trading, profit and loss account 6 months ended 31 March 1982

	£	£
Sales		880,000
O/stock raw materials	10,000	
Purchases	214,000	
	224,000	
C/stock raw materials [see workings above]	31,700	
Raw materials consumed	192,300	
Direct labour	150,000	
Prime cost	342,300	
Indirect costs	120,000	
Total factory cost	462,300	
add O/stock work in progress	3,000	
	465,300	
deduct C/stock work in progress	7,000	
Cost of completed goods	458,300	
add O/stock finished goods	7,000	
add Purchases finished goods	92,000	
	557,300	
deduct C/stock finished goods [see below]	30,390	
Cost of goods sold		526,910
Gross profit		353,090
less Selling and distribution	80,000	
Administration	40,000	
Finance	10,000	130,000
Net profit before bonus		223,090
Bonus		70,000
Net profit		153,090
Transfer to reserves	20,000	
Dividends	66,545	86,545
Retained profits		66,545

Under LIFO, the closing stock of finished goods = £25,000. This must have been

	3,500 units @ £2	= £7,000
and	7,200 units @ £2.50	= £18,000
	10,700	£25,000

Therefore, we have 10,700 units in closing stock. Under FIFO, these will be the most current purchases – i.e.

	5,000 @ £3	= £15,000
and	5,700 @ £2.70	= £15,390
	10,700	£30,390

13.8 Further exercises

Question 13.1

At the end of the financial year ended 30 April 1985 Christopher Smith, a sole trader, immediately carried out a physical stocktake. The value arrived at for closing stock was £8,000 and Christopher duly informed his accountant of the figure. His accountant swiftly produced a draft set of final accounts showing a net profit of £21,000. Following receipt of the draft accounts, Christopher Smith carried out a final review of his stock position and discovered the following facts.

(1) A single stock sheet totalling £900 had been omitted from the calculation of the total of the closing stock.
(2) Goods purchased on 14 April 1985 at a cost of £300 had been returned to a supplier on 8 May 1985.
(3) Goods with a selling price of £480 and a profit mark-up of 20 per cent on cost had been sent to a customer on a sale or return basis. Up to the time of this review the customer has not indicated whether he intends to buy the goods and no entry has been made in the accounts to record the issue of stock.
(4) Items of stock which had been valued at cost as £150 and which had been in stock for several years were now considered to be valueless.
(5) Goods which had been awaiting despatch to a customer had been included in the closing stock figure. The goods, which had cost £200, had been sold to the customer for £250 and the sale had been correctly recorded in the books.

REQUIRED

A statement showing the effect on net profit of each of the five items above, together with the adjusted overall net profit figure. [*10 marks*]

(AEB)

Answer 13.1

	£
Net profit per draft accounts	21,000
(1) add omitted stock	900
(2) no effect	
(3) add back at cost price	400
(4) deduct valueless stock	(150)
(5) deduct stock sold	(200)
Adjusted net profit	21,950

Question 13.2

A company has produced draft financial statements for the year ended 30 April 1986 which show a net profit of £108,400. Stock valuations were included as follows:

	30 April 1985	30 April 1986
Stocks of raw materials [Note 1]	£36,000	£53,000
Stocks of work in progress [Note 2]	£59,000	£45,000
Stocks of finished goods [Note 3]	£71,000	£77,000
Quantity of finished goods in stock	14,200 units	15,400 units

NOTES

(1) Raw materials consist of four separate stock items. The financial director has estimated the cost and 'net realisable value' of the four items at 30 April 1986, as follows:

Stock item	Cost £	'Net realisable value' £
1	15,000	6,000
2	10,000	15,000
3	12,000	18,000
4	10,000	14,000
	47,000	53,000

(2) The work in progress at 30 April 1985 had been overvalued by 60 per cent. No adjustment for this material error had been made in the draft accounts for the year ended 30 April 1986.

(3) It is normal policy for the company to value its stocks of finished goods on 'first in first out' (FIFO) principles. However, the stock at 30 April 1986 had been valued in error on 'last in first out' (LIFO) principles. The FIFO valuation per unit at the end of the financial year was 6 per cent higher than at the start of the year.

Prepare a statement showing the revised net profit of the company for the year ended 30 April 1986, after taking into account any necessary amendments due to notes (1) to (3) above.   [10 marks]
                                                                          (AEB)

Answer 13.2

	£
Net profit per draft accounts	108,400
Raw material adjustment after taking lower of cost or net realisable value a reduction from £53,000 to £38,000	(15,000)
Work in progress [reduction in o/stock will reduce cost of goods sold, increase profit: £59,000 × (60/160)	22,125
FIFO C/stock £71,000 × 1.06 = £75,260	
LIFO C/stock £77,000	
Reduction in valuation of c/stock	(1,740)
Revised net profit	113,785

14 Marginal Costing

14.1 Introduction

Marginal costing begins to look at costs in a way unfamiliar to many students. When applying marginal costing principles, the overriding objective is to exclude from costing any fixed or unavoidable costs. We must only consider the short-term changes in total costs which will occur when the level of business activity changes – i.e. the marginal costs.

14.2 Marginal and absorption costing

In financial accounting, stock is valued as a sum of the direct costs of making the product (wages + materials), as well as some proportion of the indirect costs (factory overheads) of making that product. Indeed, SSAP9 ('valuation of stock and work in progress') tells us to include in our valuation of stock some proportion of factory overheads. This is known as *absorption costing*. However, for management accounting purposes, where decisions are being made about future action, the *marginal costing* approach to valuation of stock should be used – i.e. only the direct or variable production costs are used in the valuation of stock. This method will lead to profit-maximising decisions being made.

14.3 Break-even analysis

The break-even analysis technique takes the concept of marginal costing one stage further. It is a technique used to determine the minimum volume of sales needed before a firm can begin to make a profit. This minimum volume (where the firm is making neither a profit nor a loss) is the *break-even point*. It can be calculated by the formula:

$$\text{break-even Volume} = \frac{\text{total fixed costs p.a.}}{\text{selling price per unit} - \text{variable cost per unit}}$$

The denominator of the fraction is also known as the 'contribution' per unit – i.e. when each unit is sold, it earns a contribution towards the firm's fixed costs. The formula calculates how many of these contributions per unit are needed in order to cover fixed costs.

The break-even point can also be expressed in terms of £s turnover. The formula for this is given by:

$$\text{break-even turnover} = \text{price per unit} \times \frac{\text{total fixed costs p.a.}}{\text{contribution per unit}}$$

In the examination, if the question is unclear as to whether it requires the volume or turnover break-even point, give both.

14.4 The break-even chart

The break-even chart is a diagrammatic representation (and method of estimating) the break-even point.

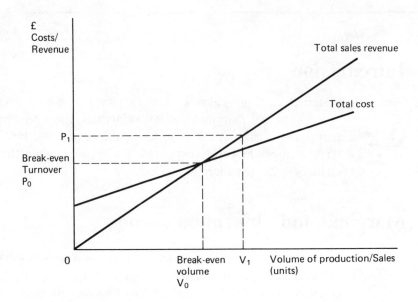

Break-even chart

The total cost line starts at zero volume of production and sales on the horizontal axis, but a certain distance up the vertical axis. This is because, even at zero level of production, a firm (in the short run) still has some *inescapable fixed costs* to meet, such as rent, rates, management costs, etc. The total cost line's slope is determined by the variable cost per unit. If you are asked to sketch a break-even chart, you only need two coordinates for the total cost line.

The first is obviously the one at zero volume with the vertical axis coordinate at the fixed cost level. The second coordinate should be the total cost for a given volume of production. For greater drawing accuracy, choose a volume at the higher end of your scale – e.g. maximum production capacity.

The total revenue line is also constructed using two pairs of coordinates. One pair of coordinates is always at (0, 0) – i.e. for zero production or sales there is zero turnover. The second pair of coordinates must be calculated by assuming a certain volume and then calculating its associated turnover by multiplying the volume by the price per unit. Again, for drawing accuracy, choose a volume close to or at full capacity.

The 'margin of safety' on the above diagram shows, for a given volume of production and sales (V_1), how much room there is for sales to fall before the firm starts to make a loss. The margin of safety can be expressed in units or £s. Notice that any volume greater than break-even volume results in a profit (since total revenue will be greater than total cost), and vice versa.

14.5 Worked examples

Example 14.1

A company started manufacturing on 1 April 1980 and incurred the following costs in its first three years:

Year ending 31 March	1981	1982	1983
	£	£	£
Raw materials	120,000	100,000	140,000
Direct labour	96,000	80,000	112,000
Variable overheads	48,000	60,000	84,000
Fixed costs	92,000	92,000	92,000

[Sales during the three years were all at £40 per unit.]

	1981	1982	1983
Production	12,000 units	10,000 units	14,000 units
Sales	10,000 units	10,000 units	15,000 units

Prepare a statement showing the gross profit for each of the three years if the company used:
(a) the marginal costing approach to valuing stock, and
(b) the absorption costing approach to valuing stock.

Solution 14.1

This question can take up too much time if the design of the layout of the solution is not considered. To save time, all three years should be in the same table.

The marginal costing approach will mean that fixed costs are treated as a 'period cost' and therefore deducted in total from revenue for the period. Absorption costing treats fixed costs as product costs (the traditional financial accounting approach).

(a)

Marginal costing statement

Year ending 31 March		1981	1982	1983
		£000s	£000s	£000s
Sales		400	400	600
Opening stock		–	44	48
Direct production costs:	Materials	120	100	140
	Labour	96	80	112
	Variable overheads	48	60	84
		264	284	384
less Closing stock [see workings]		44	48	24
Direct cost of sales		220	236	360
Contribution [Sales – Direct cost]		180	164	240
less Fixed costs		92	92	92
Gross profit		88	72	148

[Note that the opening stock of 1982 was the closing stock of 1981, etc.]

WORKINGS

Units (000's)	1981	1982	1983
Opening stock	–	2	2
add production costs	12	10	14
	12	12	16
less sales	10	10	15
Closing stock	2	2	1

$$\text{Marginal cost value of closing stock} = \frac{\text{closing units}}{\text{production units}} \times \text{direct costs for year}$$

1981	1982	1983
$\frac{2}{12} \times 264$	$\frac{2}{10} \times 240$	$\frac{1}{14} \times 336$
= 44	= 48	= 24

(b)

Absorption costing statements

Year ending 31 March		1981	1982	1983
		£000s	£000s	£000s
Sales		400	400	600
Opening stock		–	59.333	66.4
Production costs:	Materials	120	100	140
	Labour	96	80	112
	Variable overheads	48	60	84
	Fixed costs	92	92	92
		356	391.333	494.4
less Closing stock [see Workings]		59.333	66.4	30.571
Cost of sales		296.667	324.933	463.829
Gross profit		103.333	75.067	136.171

WORKINGS

$$\text{Absorption costing value of closing stock} = \frac{\text{closing stock units}}{\text{production units}} \times \text{total production}$$

costs for year

1981	1982	1983
$\frac{2}{12} \times 356$	$\frac{2}{10} \times 332$	$\frac{1}{14} \times 428$
= 59.333	= 66.4	= 30.571

Example 14.2

A company is considering its sales budget for the year ending 31 March 1986. The relevant details for the year ended 31 March 1985 are:

Units sold	100,000
Selling price	£15 per unit
Variable costs	£5.50 per unit
Fixed costs	£330,000

The members of the sales team have suggested three alternative plans to increase profits (it is expected that variable costs will remain constant per unit).

1. Increase the selling price by 10 per cent; the slight loss in sales would be compensated by the higher revenue.
2. Reduce the selling price by 5 per cent, thus increasing the demand.
3. The sales representatives should have their basic salary reduced, and instead be paid a low basic salary and a commission of 30p for each unit they sell. This would reduce fixed costs by £20,000.

You are required:
(a) to calculate the sales, in units, required by methods 1 and 2 to maintain the profit level of the year ended 31 March 1985 and
(b) to calculate the Break-even Point if suggestion 3 was adopted, and to compare this with the break-even point for the year ended 31 March 1985. [18]

(OLE)

Solution 14.2

(a)
Calculate 1985 profits:

	£
Total revenue 100,000 units at £15 =	1,500,000
Variable costs: 100,000 × £5.50 =	550,000
Contribution	950,000
Fixed costs	330,000
Profit	620,000

This is our objective profit for the year to 31 March 1986

Method (1) If the selling price is increased by 10 per cent, the new price will be £15 × 110% = £16.50. This will yield a unit contribution as follows:

	£
price	16.50
	£
variable cost	5.50
	£
contribution	11.00

If we wish to earn a profit of £620,000 after covering fixed costs of £330,000, our total contribution will have to be £950,000 (profit and fixed costs). Therefore, we will need to sell

$$\frac{£950,000}{£11.00} \left[\text{i.e.} \frac{\text{fixed costs} + \text{profit}}{\text{contribution per unit}} \right] \text{units} = 86,364 \text{ units}$$

Method (2) If the selling price is reduced by 5 per cent, this results in a new price of £14.25, and a unit contribution of £14.25 − £5.50 = £8.75. Therefore, we will need to sell £950,000/£8.75 = 108,571 units.

(b)

Using the formula

$$\text{break-even units} = \frac{\text{fixed costs}}{\text{unit contribution}}$$

for suggestion (3), we have fixed costs of £310,000 (a reduction of £20,000). However, we have an additional variable cost of 30p per unit, thus increasing variable costs to £5.50 + 30p = £5.80. This reduces the unit contribution to £15.00 − £5.80 = £9.20. Thus, break-even will be reached at £310,000/£9.20 units = 33,696 units. For 1985, the break-even point was reached at £330,000/£9.50 units = 34,737 units.

14.6   Further exercises

Question 14.1

Monteplana Ltd produced the following financial statement for the year ended 31 December 1983:

	£	£
Sales (100,000 units)		300,000
Less		
Direct materials	100,000	
Direct labour	40,000	
Variable factory overhead	10,000	
Fixed factory overhead	100,000	250,000
Manufacturing profit		50,000
Less		
Selling and distribution expenses	30,000	
Administrative expenses	30,000	60,000
Net loss		10,000

There were no opening or closing stocks of either finished goods or work-in-progress. The factory plant had a production capacity of 200,000 units per annum.

As a result of the net loss arising in 1983, the sales director maintained that the loss had arisen through not operating the plant at full capacity and that an extensive advertising campaign would increase sales significantly. Thus the board of directors agreed that £40,000 would be spent on an advertising campaign in 1984, and that the plant would be worked to full capacity, producing 200,000 units.

The following results were achieved in the financial year ended 31 December 1984.

(1) 130,000 units were sold at the 1983 price.
(2) All factory variable expenses increased directly in proportion to output.
(3) There was no increase in selling and administrative expenses except that due to increased advertising.

All the directors agreed that in order to pursue a policy of consistency, stocks of finished goods should continue to be valued at the full manufacturing unit cost.

The accountant stated that he would prefer to seek stock valuation including manufacturing variable costs only.

REQUIRED

(a) An income statement for the year ended 31 December 1984 on the agreed basis of valuing stocks. [5 marks]

(b) An alternative income statement for the year ended 31 December 1984 using the accountant's suggestion as the basis of valuing stocks. [5 marks]

(c) (i) Use accepted accountancy principles to explain the 'correctness' of the argument regarding the stock valuation of the directors.

(ii) Write a memorandum which the accountant could submit to the directors in an effort to persuade them to change to his policy for stock valuation. The memorandum should explain the shortcomings of the present policy and the advantages which would accrue from the change. [10 marks]

(d) Advise the company whether it should continue to produce to full capacity. [5 marks]

(AEB)

Answer 14.1

(a)

	£	£
Sales		390,000
less Materials	200,000	
Labour	80,000	
Variable overheads	20,000	
Fixed factory overheads	100,000	
	400,000	
less Closing stock		
[(70/200) × £400,000]	140,000	
Cost of sales		260,000
Gross profit		130,000
less Selling and distribution	70,000	
Administration	30,000	100,000
Net profit		30,000

(b)

	£	£
Sales		390,000
Total variable costs	300,000	
less Closing stock [(70/200) × £300,000]	105,000	
Direct cost of sales		195,000
Contribution		195,000
less Factory fixed costs		100,000
Factory profit		95,000
less Selling and distribution	70,000	
Administration	30,000	100,000
Net (loss)		(5,000)

137

(c)

(i) The directors' method is based on absorption costing. This follows guidelines in SSAP9 — 'valuation of stocks and work in progress'. This is fine for financial accounting but not suitable for management accounting.

(ii) From: Accountant
     To: Directors

Subject: *Stock Valuation*

The present policy of valuing stocks using absorption costing principles is fine for historic financial reporting, but is not suitable as a basis for short-term decisions on pricing and volume, etc. Such decisions should be based on marginal costing principles, which concentrate only on those costs which change in the short run.

Absorption costing carries forward a proportion of fixed factory overheads in our closing stock valuations; this has an effect of inflating reported profits whenever the volume of closing stock increases.

Marginal costing treats factory fixed costs as period costs, rather than product costs, and focuses attention on contribution earned towards these fixed costs from a given sales volume and revenue. Stocks are valued at their direct cost of production — i.e. including those costs which can be directly traced to the product cost. These are the only costs which will change as a result of decisions in the short run.

(d) The closing stock figure of 70,000 units is over 50 per cent of our volume sales of 130,000 units. I advise against producing at full capacity of 200,000 units, if our sales volume is expected to remain at the same level next year.

Question 14.2

A company manufacturing one type of commodity, selling at £15 per unit, has the capacity to produce 30,000 units. The budget for the year ending 31 December 1984 predicts sales of 28,000 units.

The costs of each unit are expected to be:

Wages	£3.00
Materials	£5.00
Overheads	£2.00

Fixed costs for the year are expected to be £130,000.

1. Calculate the break-even point for sales for the year.
2. What profit can be expected during the year, assuming that the opening and closing stocks remain constant?
3. If management are willing to invest £100,000 with an expected return of 20 per cent, how many units must be produced to achieve this?
4. If, by reducing the selling price to £13, extra sales can be expected, what must the volume of production and sales be to achieve the same profits as in (3) above?   [*18*]

(OLE)

Answer 14.2

1. Break-even = $\dfrac{£130,000}{£15 - £10}$ = 26,000 units.

2. Sales 28,000 units.

   Contribution per unit = £5

Total contribution	£140,000
less Fixed costs	£130,000
Profit	£ 10,000

3. Desired profit = 20% of £100,000 = £20,000

   Required units = $\dfrac{\text{fixed costs} + \text{profit}}{\text{unit contribution}}$ = $\dfrac{£130,000 + £20,000}{£5}$

   = 30,000 units

4. If the price falls to £13, the contribution will fall to £3:

   Required units = $\dfrac{£150,000}{3}$ = 50,000 units

15 Costing For Decision-making

15.1 Relevant costs

The subject matter of this chapter is closely allied to that of Chapter 14, marginal costing. It is costing for decision-making using the concept of marginality — i.e. 'What costs and/or revenues will change as a result of the decision made?'

We must concentrate only on changes. We must ignore those costs that will not change in the short run. These non-changing costs may have a variety of accounting labels.

(i) *Fixed costs* Costs which do not change with a change in the level of output or turnover.
(ii) *Sunk costs* Expenditure on items already incurred. For example, the firm may have surplus stocks of a raw material, bought and paid for a while ago. If it has only one use for this material, its use will now have a zero cost.
(iii) *Inescapable costs* Costs which the firm will incur regardless of its decision. For example, it is committed to a basic wage of £80 per week for 10 men. If for some reason it cannot decrease the number of men, or basic wage, it has inescapable cost of £800 per week.

15.2 'Make or buy' decisions

This is a popular question topic. It uses the concept of marginality. It should, however, be treated with caution. We have the pure quantitative calculations and recommendations, but there is a need to be aware of the non-financial consequences of decisions.

For example, suppose that a firm has the following costs of production for a component it needs in a finished product:

materials — £2 per unit
labour — £5 per unit
departmental overheads — £3 per unit (allocated on the basis of man-hours worked as a proportion of total man-hours)

The firm has established that a subcontractor could supply the component at £9 per unit. Should the firm make or buy?

Well, we must look at the costs which will change as a result of buying-in the component. How much will the firm save?

(i) It will save materials of £2 per unit.
(ii) It will probably save labour of £5 per unit.
(iii) It will *not* save the departmental overheads.

These are fixed costs, which have been allocated to the product, but they are *not* direct costs. Therefore, by discontinuing production it will save £2 + £5 = £7 per unit for every unit it buys in, but it will have to pay £9 per unit to the subcontractor. Therefore, it will cost £2 more to buy-in than to make itself. Therefore, the firm should reject the offer on numerical/financial grounds. However, it should consider such areas as (a) the quality of its own production compared with that of the subcontractor; (b) any alternative uses to which the raw materials and/or labour could be put.

15.3 Pricing

Questions in the area of pricing concentrate on minimum pricing or break-even pricing — i.e. for a given volume of sales, what price should the firm set in order to break-even? Here we need to remember the basic equation or definition of break-even: total costs = total revenue, where total costs = fixed costs + variable costs, and total revenue = volume × sales price per unit.

Therefore, if we are given all of these except the price, then break-even price is simply

$$\frac{\text{fixed costs} + \text{variable costs}}{\text{volume}}$$

Another examination topic is that of acceptance or rejection of additional sales orders — i.e. a firm receives a special order, but at a price which is considerably below its 'normal' selling price. Should the firm accept the order? Well, on purely financial grounds the firm should accept the order as long as it yields an additional *contribution* towards its fixed costs, even if that contribution is only small. We must ignore any fixed or inescapable costs, and concentrate on the *relevant* costs of satisfying that additional order.

However, there are non-financial considerations to 'marginal-cost pricing'. By selling an additional order at a price just above its marginal cost, the firm may well be running the risk of alienating its existing customers, to whom it has supplied a product priced on a full-cost (including overheads) basis. The firm must make sure (from a marketing strategy/trade relations aspect) that if it supplies at a price well below the 'normal price', the product is not distributed in the same geographic market as that of its current customers, or, if it is, that it is sold under a different brand name, with its own distinctive labelling/packaging. This is how many large supermarkets are able to sell 'own-label' products alongside 'proprietary brand' products, even though both products are made by the same manufacturer.

15.4 Contraction

The firm may be operating several branches or perhaps several product lines. The reported accounting statements show that some of them appear to be running at a loss. Should they close down all or some of the loss-making areas, and how will this decision affect the firm's profit? Once again, we must concentrate only on those costs which change as a result of our decision/recommendation. The first thing to do is to rearrange or re-format the accounting statements into 'operating' statements, which will show the contribution earned by each area of operations. Any area yielding a positive contribution should be kept going, unless there is an alternative use of those resources (opportunity cost) which would yield a greater contribution than that at present.

An operating statement for a branch-closure decision would be as follows:

| | Branch | | | Total |
	A £000s	B £000s	C £000s	£000s
Turnover	40	30	16	86
Cost of sales	20	15	8	43
Trading profit	20	15	8	43
less Direct costs				
Branch staff	7	5	5	17
other Fixed costs directly incurred by the branch				
[rates, phone]	4	3	2	9
Contribution	9	7	1	17
Head office costs				10
Profit				7

Here each branch is earning a contribution. If, say, C were to be closed down, the firm would lose C's £1,000 contribution, which would result in the firm's net profit reducing to £6,000. Notice that when head office costs are 'allocated' to the branches, the effect is to reduce the reported 'profits' of each branch.

If £3,000 of the head office costs had been allocated to C, it would appear that C was operating at a loss. This might lead to a decision to close C down. This would lead to the firm's profit falling to £6,000, since the allocated £3,000 of head office costs are 'inescapable' – i.e. they will still be incurred, regardless of whether C is open or closed.

15.5 Worked examples

Example 15.1

A company currently makes and sells 1,000 units per month of its product. The selling price is £55 per unit, and unit costs are: direct labour £3; direct materials £7; variable overheads £4. Fixed costs per month are £16,200.

The firm receives two special export orders for completion in the same month. Order A requests 500 units at a special price of £6,500; order B requires 600 units at £12,000. Order A will require no special treatment, but order B will demand extra processing at a cost of £5 per unit. The firm has sufficient productive capacity to undertake either A or B in addition to its current production.

(a) Show the firm's profits for the month if
   (i) normal production only takes place
  (ii) order A is accepted
  (iii) order B is accepted   [12 marks]
(b) Explain why a company will generally accept an order which makes a positive contribution towards overheads.   [8 marks]
(c) Before accepting an order based upon marginal cost prices, what safeguards must a firm adopt?   [5 marks]

Solution 15.1

It is important to concentrate on 'contribution' throughout this question.

(a) (i)

Monthly operating statement for normal production only

			£
Sales	1000 @ £55		55,000
Variable costs:	Labour	£3	
	Materials	£7	
	Overheads	£4	
	1,000 ×	£14	14,000
Contribution			41,000
less Fixed costs			16,200
Profit			24,800

(ii) If order A is accepted (in addition to the normal 1,000 units), the firm will earn its normal contribution on the 1,000 units, plus the additional contribution on the extra 500 units from order A. Therefore, profit for the month will be:

	£
Sales from order A	6,500
less Direct costs of order A [500 × £14]	7,000
A yields a negative contribution of	(500)
add Contribution from normal production	41,000
Net contribution	40,500
less Fixed costs	16,200
Profit	24,300

(iii) If order B is accepted, profit for the month will be:

	£
Sales from order B	12,000
less Direct costs of order B	
600 units @ £14 + additional £5 = £19	11,400
Contribution from order B	600
add Contribution from normal production	41,000
Net contribution	41,600
less Fixed costs	16,200
Profit	25,400

(b) The company will generally accept an order which yields a positive contribution, since any positive contribution will increase overall company profits (or reduce company losses). Where the company has a choice between alternative orders, it should obviously choose the order which makes the greatest contribution, since this will lead to profit maximisation.

(c) Before accepting an order based on marginal cost prices, the firm should ensure that the distribution of that order does not take place in its home market, since this will lead to antagonism and loss of goodwill from its home market distributors.

Example 15.2

The firm Retailers Ltd operates a grocery business with a large shop in Riverdale and a small shop in the village of Fairvale. The draft accounts of Retailers for the year ended 31 May 1984 are as follows:

	Riverdale		Fairvale	
	£	£	£	£
Sales		250,000		50,000
Cost of sales		196,000		44,000
Gross profit		54,000		6,000
Manager's salary	8,000		5,000	
Other staff salaries	17,000		4,000	
Rates	3,500		1,200	
Motor van expenses	1,000		1,000	
Rent			600	
General expenses	6,000		1,200	
Depreciation				
Fixtures	3,000		500	
Motor van	800	39,300	800	14,300
Net profit (loss)		14,700		(8,300)

The above figures follow similar results over recent years and Mr Jones, the manager of Retailers, is considering the future of the Fairvale branch. The following additional information is available.

(1) The Riverdale shop is responsible for the administration of the business and for ordering and handling all of the goods sold by the Fairvale shop. A handling charge of 10 per cent on cost has been added to the Fairvale cost of sales figure and the same amount deducted from the Riverdale cost of sales.

(2) During the past three years the Fairvale premises have been rented on an annual basis only. The landlord of the premises now insists on a 10-year lease being introduced from 1 June 1984 at an annual rent of £2,500 per annum.

(3) The fixtures at the Fairvale shop, purchased for £10,000, have been depreciated by £4,000 at 31 May 1984, using the straight line method of depreciation.

(4) Although the motor van is used for delivery to the Fairvale shop, the van will continue to be required by the Riverdale branch. However, the closure of the Fairvale shop will result in an expected saving of £400 on vehicle running costs.

(5) Apart from Mr Jones who manages both branches, the Fairvale shop is staffed by part-time assistants. A closure of the Fairvale shop would enable Mr Jones to work fully at Riverdale and reduce other staff salaries at Riverdale by £1,500 per year.

(6) General expenses are allocated between Riverdale and Fairvale on the basis of turnover. It is estimated that a total saving of £500 on general expenses would result from the closure of the Fairvale shop.

(7) Just over twelve months ago Mr Smith, a redundant sales executive, offered to purchase the Fairvale shop from Retailers Ltd, the consideration being £1,000 for the fixtures and to purchase the stock at cost. Mr Smith has recently approached Mr Jones again but on learning of the rent increase is prepared to purchase only the stock at cost. Apart from Mr Smith, an active member of the Fairvale Village Association who is determined that the village's only remaining shop will not close, it is unlikely that the shop will be taken over by anyone else.

REQUIRED

(a) Calculate the profit which would have accrued to Retailers Ltd for the year ended 31 May 1984 had the sale to Mr Smith been completed on 1 June 1983.   [*13 marks*]

(b) Advise Retailers Ltd whether to accept Mr Smith's second offer. [*8 marks*]

(c) Consider the implications for the community of Fairvale of closing the shop. [*4 marks*]

(AEB)

Solution 15.2

(a) This part of the question concentrates on those costs and revenues which would have changed if Fairvale had closed a year ago.

Trading, profit and loss account year to 31 May 1984 (if Fairvale had closed)

	£	£
Sales		250,000
Cost of Sales [Note 1]		200,000
Gross profit		50,000
Manager's salary [Note 2]	13,000	
Other staff salaries [Note 3]	15,500	
Rates	3,500	
Motor van expenses [Note 4]	1,600	
General expenses [Note 5]	6,700	
Depreciation of fixtures	3,000	
Depreciation of van	1,600	44,900
Net profit		5,100

NOTES

(1) Reduce Fairvale cost of sales by $\frac{1}{11}$ for administration charges = £4,000 and add back onto Riverdale (£196,000 + £4,000 = £200,000).

(2) The manager will still receive the same salary, even though one branch is closed.

(3) No staff at Fairvale but a saving of £1,500 at Riverdale (£17,000 − £1,500 = £15,500).

(4) Previous cost £2,000 p.a., less saving of £400.

(5) Total general expenses £7,200, less saving of £500.

(b) What we are asked to consider here is really whether Retailers Ltd should close the Fairvale shop down, in the light of the rent increase. The fact that Mr Jones will buy the stock at cost is not relevant.

Let us look at the contribution that Fairvale will make in the next twelve months to Retailers' overheads, assuming the same level of activity.

	£	£	
Sales		50,000	
Cost of sales		40,000	
Trading profit		10,000	
less Staff salaries	4,000		
Rates	1,200		
Motor expenses	400		[this is what would be saved if Fairvale closed]
Rent	2,500		
General expenses	500		[as motor expenses]
Depreciation on fixtures	500		
Depreciation on motor van	−		[this will not change]
Potential staff saving at Riverdale	1,500		

$$\underline{10,600}$$

Negative contribution to company overheads $\underline{(600)}$

On the basis of the above statement, it would be financially wise for the Fairvale shop to close, since, with the increased rent, it earns a negative contribution of £600 towards Retailers Ltd's overheads.

(c) Implications of closing: (i) loss of part-time employment for local people; (ii) loss of shopping convenience; (iii) possible idle shop premises.

Example 15.3

Weston, a manufacturer operating in a rural area of high unemployment, was reviewing the manufacture of three components M, P and Q, which form part of the single product manufactured. The following information has been extracted from the budget prepared for the next financial year.

	M £	P £	Q £
Direct Materials	75,000	160,000	88,000
Direct Labour	25,000	40,000	24,000
Variable Overheads	25,000	100,000	40,000
Direct Costs	125,000	300,000	152,000
Fixed Overheads attributable to components	10,000	8,000	12,000
Annual Production in units	5,000	10,000	8,000

The fixed overheads shown above are known to be incurred as a direct consequence of the production of the components.

Enquiries have been made with a view to the possibility of buying in these components, and a potential supplier has quoted the following prices per unit:

M £19   P £32   Q £16

If the parts were bought in, it would involve additional handling charges annually as follows:

M £2,500   P £3,000   Q £3,200

The cessation of production of the components would mean that twelve skilled workmen would be made redundant; no redundancy payment would be incurred. In the face of this threat, the trade union officials have submitted suggestions which, if implemented, would save the following amounts in direct costs:

M	£20,000
P	£10,000
Q	£16,000

They have also indicated that they would give serious consideration to co-operation in other cost-saving investigations.

REQUIRED

On the assumption that budget levels will be achieved,

(a) a detailed forecast statement (preferably in columnar form) showing the savings or extra cost which would arise should the management decide to purchase the components from the quoted supplier;   *[11 marks]*

(b) a report to the management of the firm indicating whether all or any of the components should continue to be manufactured within the factory.

Your report should include factors which should be considered by the management other than profit savings or losses. *[14 marks]*

(AEB)

Solution 15.3

(a) This is a 'make or buy' decision, where we turn our attention to the extra costs or savings achieved by buying in the components. First we must restate our budgeted costs, assuming that we continue to make all three components *and* that the savings in direct costs are implemented.

Budgeted production costs	M	P	Q
Number of units	5,000	10,000	8,000
Direct costs	£105,000	£290,000	£136,000
Fixed overheads	£10,000	£8,000	£12,000
Total cost	£115,000	£298,000	£148,000

Costs of buying in	M	P	Q
Number of units	5,000	10,000	8,000
Cost per unit	£19	£32	£16
Total direct cost	£95,000	£320,000	£128,000
Extra handling charges	£2,500	£3,000	£3,200
	£97,500	£323,000	£131,200
Total cost saving/(extra cost)	£17,500	(£25,000)	£16,800

(b)

Report

Subject: Make or buy components M, P, Q

In the light of recent forecasts, it appears that in the short run it would be more profitable for Weston to discontinue production of components M and Q, thereby making an annual saving of £17,500 on M and £16,800 on Q, on the basis of the budgeted volumes. However, we should consider the following:

  (i) Can we rely on delivery from outside suppliers?

 (ii) Could we replace or re-hire our redundant skilled workers if, for some reason, it became necessary to restart production of M and Q?

(iii) What additional cost savings could be made to our current production costs?

(iv) How reliable are the unions' cost-saving projections?

15.6 Further exercises

Question 15.1

(a) Explain the 'contribution' principle and give one example of a situation where it would be most useful.

(b) Exwyzed plc has a production capacity of 24,000 units. The budget for the next financial year is:

	£	£
Sales (20,000 units at £15)		300,000
less Raw Materials	80,000	
Wages	35,000	
Variable overheads	22,000	
Depreciation	26,000	
Other fixed costs	30,000	
Manager's commission	30,000	223,000
Profit		77,000

The manager's commission is directly related to units sold.

According to market research, it would be possible to sell abroad the extra 4,000 units that the factory has the capacity to produce, if they could be sold for £10 per unit.

The directors are considering this and a suggestion made by one of the board that if the selling price were reduced by 10 per cent, all the products could be sold in the existing market. To boost sales an advertising campaign would have to be mounted, with a possible cost of £4,000.

You are required to advise the directors which course of action to take, supporting your advice with the relevant figures. [18]

(Oxford)

Answer 15.1

(a) See the text.
(b) Budgeted operating statement if 4,000 units are sold abroad:

	£	£
Sales [20,000 @ 15 and 4,000 @ £10] =		340,000
less Raw materials [+20%]	96,000	
Wages [+20%]	42,000	
Variable overheads [+20%]	26,400	
Manager's commission [+20%]	36,000	200,400
Contribution		139,600
Depreciation		26,000
Other fixed costs		30,000
Profit		83,600

Budgeted operating statement if prices reduced by 10 per cent:

	£	£
Sales [24,000 @ £13.50]		324,000
direct costs [as above]	200,400	
plus additional advertising	4,000	204,400
Contribution		119,600
Depreciation		26,000
Other fixed costs		30,000
Profit		63,600

From the above, I would advise the firm to adopt the first suggestion of selling the excess production abroad. This will increase profits by £83,600 –

£77,000 = £6,600 next year. The proposal to reduce the price by 10 per cent and increase advertising does in fact lead to even lower profits than the original budget, cutting them by £13,400 (£77,000 − £63,600).

Question 15.2

Kilgant and Company, a car-hire firm, has three depots in a very large city area of the country. The depots may be categorised as 'outer', 'inner' and 'central'. The following information has been drawn from the accounts for the six months ended 30 September 1983 by a new owner of the business:

	Outer £	Inner £	Central £	Total £
Income from hire shops	60,000	190,000	460,000	710,000
Variable costs	34,000	72,000	180,000	286,000
Fixed costs −				
depots	4,000	8,000	8,000	20,000
car fleet	16,000	32,000	32,000	80,000
central garages, and				
administration	34,000	68,000	68,000	170,000
	88,000	180,000	288,000	556,000
Profit/(Loss)	(28,000)	10,000	172,000	154,000

Other data

	Outer	Inner	Central	Total
Mileage	400,000	300,000	600,000	1,300,000
Number of cars	20	40	40	100

The new owner, formerly a building contractor operating from one 'yard' only, is perturbed by the reported loss from the depot in the outer region and has formulated the following proposals and forecasts, all of which relate to this depot.

(1) Close the depot, and thus avoid the depot and car fleet fixed costs.
(2) Increase income by doubling all the hire charges: it is forecast that the number of people hiring cars will decrease by 60 per cent.
(3) Increase income by reducing hire charges by 20 per cent so that an estimated 40 per cent more people will hire cars.
(4) Reduce the number of cars by 8 (which will not be replaced in next year's renewal programme): it is forecast that mileage will be reduced by 160,000 miles and income by £24,000.
Note. Forecasts have assumed that percentage increases and decreases in the number of people using hire cars results in proportionate changes in revenue and related costs.

REQUIRED

(a) The profit (or loss) Kilgant and Company may expect to make in a six months trading period under each of the proposals given in (1), (2), (3) and (4) above.   [*18 marks*]
(b) State what other considerations need to be taken into account before a final decision is taken.   [*7 marks*]

(AEB)

Answer 15.2

(a) Once again we must look at contribution and additional costs or savings. First, let us restate the information given, relating to the 'outer' depot.

		£
Income from charges		60,000
Variable costs		34,000
Contribution to depot overheads		26,000
Depot overheads:		
	£	
depot	4,000	
car fleet	16,000	20,000
Contribution to Head Office overheads		6,000

If proposal (1) is adopted, we shall lose the £6,000 contribution earned, and therefore the total company profit will fall to £148,000 assuming no overhead savings.

Proposal (2), to double hire charges, with consequent reduction of 60 per cent volume, will have the following effect:

	£
Turnover [£60,000 × 2 × 0.4]	48,000
Variable costs [£34,000 × 0.4]	13,600
Contribution to depot overheads	34,400

The contribution will increase by £8,400, thus increasing the total company profit to £154,000 + £8,400 = £162,400.

Proposal (3), to reduce hire charges by 20 per cent, will have the following effect:

	£
Turnover £60,000 × 0.8 × 1.4	67,200
Variable costs £34,000 × 1.4	47,600
Contribution to depot overheads	19,600

This reduces the contribution by £26,000 − £19,600 = £6,400, and reduces the total company profit to £147,600.

Proposal (4), to reduce the number of cars by 8, and mileage by 160,000 miles, will have the following effects:

	£	£
Turnover		36,000
Variable costs $[£34,000 \times \frac{400-160}{400}]$		20,400
Contribution to depot overheads		15,600
Depot	4,000	
Car fleet $[£16,000 \times \frac{20-8}{20}] =$	9,600	13,600
Contribution to Head Office overheads		2,000

This reduces the contribution by £4,000 and therefore the total company profits would fall to £150,000.

(b) Other considerations:

   (i) accuracy of forecast;

  (ii) peculiarities of last six months' trading conditions;

 (iii) possible redistribution of fleet to other depots and consequent effect on profits;

 (iv) method of pricing – perhaps hire charges should include an element of a mileage charge.

16 Budgeting

16.1 Introduction

Questions on budgeting usually require an application of common-sense and a clear interpretation of the question. The biggest problem with these questions is that they tend to be rather time-consuming. It is essential that a clear layout be produced, so that it is easy to read, and avoidable errors are not made.

All budgeting questions concern time (usually in months), and timing delays between sales and receipts and between purchases and payments. Look carefully for information concerning periods of credit. If a firm allows two months credit, sales made in January will not become receipts until March.

16.2 Subsidiary budgets

There are many types of subsidiary budgets, such as raw materials stock, production, debtors, creditors and cash.

The raw materials stock and production budgets can be expressed in terms of physical units, or in money measurement. A physical unit budget will allow the firm to forecast how many units it will have in stock at the end of each month and whether this will be sufficient to support the budgeted level of production or sales. If stock falls to zero, we have an 'out-of-stock' position, which will have to be corrected by the firm. When preparing a stock budget, you must determine whether the budget required is for units or monetary value.

A physical stock budget for finished goods will have the following format:

	Jan.	Feb.	...	Dec.
Opening stock				
add Units produced	——			
less Units sold	——			
= Closing stock				

Remember that the closing stock for January will become the opening stock for February, etc.

A debtors budget will have the following format

	Jan.	Feb.	...	Dec.
Balance b/d				
add Credit sales	——			
less Receipts	——			
Balance c/d				

Again the balance at the end of January becomes the balance at the beginning of February.

16.3 The master budget

'Master budget' is simply another name for a forecast trading profit and loss account for the whole period, and uses aggregate figures for sales, purchases and expenses, as detailed in the subsidiary budgets. The opening and closing stock figures are taken from the stock budget – i.e. stock at the beginning of the budgeted period and stock at the end of the budgeted period.

16.4 The forecast balance sheet

Most of the figures for assets and liabilities are taken from the closing balance figures of the subsidiary budgets – e.g. debtors, creditors, cash, stock. The capital will be the capital from the last balance sheet, plus forecast net profit, less any forecast drawings (for a sole trader) or less any forecast dividends (for a limited company). Fixed assets must, of course, be updated to take account of acquisitions/disposals and depreciation for the budgeted period.

16.5 Worked examples

Example 16.1

The Balance Sheet of J. Walker at 31 December 1982 is as follows:

			£
Capital			952,000
Loan			15,000
			£967,000
Fixed Assets at Book value			924,700
Investments			42,000
		£	
Stocks – Finished Goods (1,000 units)		8,500	
— Raw Materials		12,000	
Debtors		80,000	
		100,500	
	£		
Creditors – Raw Materials	46,000		
Fixed Expenses	1,800		
Bank	52,400	100,200	300
			£967,000

The forecast figures for the six months ending 30 June 1983 are as follows:
(*a*) Production is expected to be

	Jan.	Feb.	Mar.	Apr.	May	June
Units	8,000	10,000	9,000	7,000	8,000	9,000

(*b*) Expected Sales:

Units	7,000	8,000	9,000	10,000	8,000	7,000

(*c*) The selling price of all goods is expected to be £20 per unit.

(d) Production costs are forecast to be £12 per unit, with total fixed costs £24,000 per annum. The variable costs other than raw materials are paid in the month that they are incurred.

(e) Raw materials purchases are expected to be:

Jan.	Feb.	Mar.	April	May	June
£57,000	£81,000	£72,600	£57,300	£63,000	£75,000

(f) 50 per cent of the sales are expected to be for cash and 50 per cent of the debtors pay during the month following sale. The remainder usually take 2 months to pay.

(g) Raw materials used in production are expected to cost £8 per unit.

(h) Purchases are all on credit and are paid for in three equal monthly instalments by special arrangements with the suppliers. The first instalment is paid in the month of purchase.

(i) The fixed expenses are spread evenly over the year and are paid one month after they are incurred.

(j) Other expenses of the business are expected to be £4,800 per month and are paid in the month that they are incurred.

(k) Depreciation is to be written off the fixed assets of £21,000 for the year.

(l) Dividends on investments of £4,200 are expected in mid-April.

(m) Of the debtors at 31 December 1982, £20,000 are for November sales and £12,000 of creditors are for November purchases.

(n) Total creditors at 30 June 1983 are £73,000 and stock of finished goods £32,500.

You are required to prepare for the six months to 30 June 1983:
  (i) A Raw Materials Stock Budget
  (ii) A Cash Budget
  (iii) An account to find the Net Profit
and (iv) A Balance Sheet at 30 June 1983.   [40]
(OLE)

Solution 16.1

(i) The raw material stock budget is a straightforward procedure. Note (g) in the question tells us that, for every unit of production, £8 worth of raw materials will be used up. Note also that we have an opening stock of £12,000 of raw materials, as shown in the 31 December 1982 balance sheet. We must remember that the closing stock of one month is the opening stock of the next month.

Raw Materials Stock Budget, January–June 1983

	Jan. £	Feb. £	Mar. £	Apr. £	May £	June £
Opening stock	12,000	5,000	6,000	6,600	7,900	6,900
add Purchases [Note e]	57,000	81,000	72,600	57,300	63,000	75,000
	69,000	86,000	78,600	63,900	70,900	81,900
less Consumption [Notes a, g]	64,000	80,000	72,000	56,000	64,000	72,000
Closing stock	5,000	6,000	6,600	7,900	6,900	9,900

(ii) The cash budget will take considerably longer to draft. We must concentrate on timing of receipts and payments, rather than sales purchases, expenses, etc. We can first draft a receipts schedule, then a payments schedule and finally a summarised cash budget.

The receipts of J. Walker consist of cash sales, receipts from debtors, and dividends from investments (note that the investments are shown as an asset in the balance sheet).

The selling price of each unit is £20 (note c); thus the value of sales in January is £20 × 7,000 units = £140,000. 50 per cent are for cash. The balance is paid in two halves — one in February one in March (note f).

Receipts schedule January–June 1983

	£	£	£	£	£	£
Cash sales [Notes b, f]	70,000	80,000	90,000	100,000	80,000	70,000

	Jan.	Feb.	Mar.	Apr.	May	June
	£	£	£	£	£	£
Cash sales [Notes b, f]	70,000	80,000	90,000	100,000	80,000	70,000
One-month debtors	30,000*	35,000	40,000	45,000	50,000	40,000
Two-month debtors	20,000*	30,000*	35,000	40,000	45,000	50,000
Dividends				4,200		
Total	120,000	145,000	165,000	189,200	175,000	160,000

*Note (m) tells us that, of the December debtors, £20,000 is from November sales. These will be two months old by the end of January, and will therefore pay in January. This leaves £80,000–£20,000 = £60,000 of debtors, which must be due to December sales. 50 per cent of these will pay in January (£30,000) and the other 50 per cent in February. This pattern is repeated throughout the budget.

The payments schedule will have a larger variety of items than the receipts. This is only to be expected. Again we must concentrate on timing delays. We must remember that depreciation (note k) is *not* a cash flow.

Payments to trade creditors are straightforward — e.g. January purchases are £57,000 (note e). One-third is paid in January (£19,000) and £19,000 in February and £19,000 in March. On this basis, trade creditors at the end of June should be $\frac{1}{3}$ of May purchases ($\frac{1}{3}$ of £63,000 = £21,000), plus $\frac{2}{3}$ of June ($\frac{2}{3}$ of £75,000 = £50,000), total £71,000. However, note (a) tells us that total creditors at the end of June are £73,000, which is a further £2,000! This can only be the amount owing for fixed expenses (note i). Therefore, fixed expenses will be £2,000 per month, paid one month late.

Production costs per unit are £12 (note d). Of this, £8 is for raw materials (note g). Therefore, the remaining £4 is for labour and other variable overheads.

Payments schedule January–June 1983

	Jan.	Feb.	Mar.	Apr.	May	June
	£	£	£	£	£	£
Trade creditors 0 month	19,000	27,000	24,200	19,100	21,000	25,000
1 month	17,000*	19,000	27,000	24,200	19,100	21,000
2 months	12,000*	17,000*	19,000	27,000	24,200	19,100
Other variable costs [£4]	32,000	40,000	36,000	28,000	32,000	36,000
Fixed expenses	1,800	2,000	2,000	2,000	2,000	2,000
Other expenses [note j]	4,800	4,800	4,800	4,800	4,800	4,800
Total	86,600	109,800	113,000	105,100	103,100	107,900

*Note m.

Notice the diagonal pattern of payments to creditors. This is an easy way to build up the schedule, rather than trying to complete all of the payments for one month before moving on to the next month.

The cash budget can now be completed in summary form.

Cash budget January–June 1983

	Jan. £	Feb. £	Mar. £	Apr. £	May £	June £
Balance b/d	(52,400)*	(19,000)	16,200	68,200	152,300	224,200
add Receipts	120,000	145,000	165,000	189,200	175,000	160,000
	67,600	126,000	181,200	257,400	327,300	384,200
deduct Payments	86,600	109,800	113,000	105,100	103,100	107,900
Balance c/d	(19,000)	16,200	68,200	152,300	224,200	276,300

*Note that the opening cash balance is an overdraft, since it is shown with liabilities in the balance sheet. We can use the conventional parentheses to show a negative figure.

(iii) An account to show the net profit can be called the master budget – i.e. a forecast trading, profit and loss account.

Forecast Trading, profit and loss account 6 months to 30 June 1983

	£	£
Sales [49,000 units at £20]		980,000
Opening stock finished goods [1,000 units]	8,500	
Production [51,000 @ £12]	612,000	
	620,500	
Closing stock [Note n]	32,500	
Direct cost of goods sold	588,000	
add Indirect manufacturing costs:		
Fixed expenses* [6 months at £2,000]	12,000	
Depreciation* [6 months]	10,500	610,500
Gross profit		369,500
Less other expenses [6 × £4,800]		28,800
add Investment income		4,200
Net profit		344,900

*Assuming these relate only to manufacturing, and assuming that closing stock is valued on a marginal cost basis.

(iv) The balance sheet needs only a few calculations.

(a) Add net profit to previous capital (there are no drawings):

Capital b/d	952,000
add Net profit	344,900
Capital c/d	1,296,900

(b) Debtors are $\frac{1}{2}$ June sales $= \frac{1}{2} \times 7,000 \times £20 = $ £70,000

and

$\frac{1}{4}$ of May sales $\quad = \frac{1}{4} \times 8,000 \times £20 = $ 40,000

110,000

	£	£	£
Fixed assets [£924,700 − £10,500)			914,200
Investments			42,000
			956,200
Current assets			
Stock − Finished goods	32,500		
− Raw materials	9,900		
Debtors	110,000		
Bank	276,300	428,700	
Creditors [note n]		73,000	
Working capital			355,700
Total Assets less Current liabilities			1,311,900
Loan			15,000
Net Assets			1,296,900
Capital			1,296,900

Example 16.2

Richard Norman commenced business on 1 November 1985, taking over the following assets and liabilities of Carr Ltd at their book value on that date:

	£
Fixed assets at cost	8,000
Depreciation − fixed assets	4,000
Stock at cost	2,000
Debtors	4,000
Creditors	3,000
Bank overdraft	1,000
General expenses accrued	100

In addition to his payment to the shareholders of Carr Ltd, Norman paid £10,000 into the business bank account on 1 November 1985. The debtors and creditors figures relate to sales and purchases for the month of October 1985.

Forecasts and plans for the four months to 28 February 1986 were as follows.

(1) Gross profit will be at a constant rate of $33\frac{1}{3}\%$ of sales.
(2) Sales will be £6,000 per month in November and December, £13,500 in January and £12,000 in February. Although in the past sales have been on one month's credit, Norman will extend the credit period to two months on all sales from 1 November 1985.
(3) Norman proposes to exercise a strict control over stock levels and to organise his purchases so that his rate of stock turnover for each month is 2. All purchases will be made on terms of one month's credit.
(4) Wages will be £500 per month payable on the last day of the month.
(5) General expenses will be £400 per month: one-eighth of the general expenses are outstanding at the end of each month.
(6) Rent for the year ending 31 October 1986 will be £1,500 and will be payable on 1 June 1986.
(7) Norman, having opened asset and depreciation accounts with the balances taken over, decided to continue depreciation at the rate of 10 per cent per annum on cost on all assets in use at the end of the financial year.
(8) During December new fixed assets will be purchased for £3,000 cash and an asset which had been purchased on 1 November 1983 at a cost of £800 will be sold for £200 cash.

157

(a) A stock budget for the four months ending 28 February 1986 showing clearly the stock held at the end of each month. [*11 marks*]

(b) A cash budget for the four months ending 28 February 1986 showing clearly the bank balance at the end of each month. [*9 marks*]

(c) A forecast trading and profit and loss account for the four months ending 28 February 1986 for Richard Norman. [*5 marks*]

(AEB)

Solution 16.2

This question is only slightly different from the previous one. It requires an understanding of gross margin (gross profit as a percentage of sales), and its link with the cost of goods sold. (Sales = gross profit + cost of goods sold.) It also requires an understanding of stock turnover, since note (3) states that the rate of stock turnover for each month will be 2 – i.e.

$$\frac{\text{cost of goods sold}}{\text{average monthly stock}} = 2$$

(a) Before we can draft the stock budget, we need to calculate opening and closing stock, using the information about gross margin and stock turnover. If the gross margin is $33\frac{1}{3}\%$ of sales, it follows that the cost of goods sold is $66\frac{2}{3}\%$ of sales. Thus, we have the following schedule:

	Nov. £	Dec. £	Jan. £	Feb. £
Sales [Note 2]	6,000	6,000	13,500	12,000
∴ Cost of goods sold [$\frac{2}{3}$]	4,000	4,000	9,000	8,000

We are told that the opening stock in November is £2,000. The rate of stock turnover must be 2 [Note 3] – i.e.

$$\frac{\text{cost of goods sold}}{\text{average stock}} = 2$$

where

$$\text{average stock} = \frac{\text{opening stock} + \text{closing stock}}{2}$$

For November we have cost of goods sold = £4,000. Therefore, the average stock must be £4,000 ÷ 2 = £2,000. If the opening stock is £2,000, it follows that the closing stock must be £2,000. Thus, we can establish, on this basis, the following opening and closing stock figures:

	Nov. £	Dec. £	Jan. £	Feb. £
Cost of goods sold	4,000	4,000	9,000	8,000
Opening stock	2,000	2,000	2,000	7,000
Closing stock	2,000	2,000	7,000	1,000

(Closing stock for January must be £7,000, since the average must be £9,000 ÷ 2 = £4,500.)

158

We are now in a position to produce the stock budget. The only missing figures are for purchases, which are inserted 'by deduction' (work up from bottom):

R. Norman: Stock budget

	Nov. £	Dec. £	Jan. £	Feb. £
Opening stock	2,000	2,000	2,000	7,000
add Purchases	4,000	4,000	14,000	2,000
	6,000	6,000	16,000	9,000
less Cost of goods sold	4,000	4,000	9,000	8,000
= Closing stock	2,000	2,000	7,000	1,000

(b) Time can be saved by drafting the cash budget straight away, rather than producing receipt and payments schedules first.

R. Norman: Cash budget

	Nov. £	Dec. £	Jan. £	Feb. £
Balance b/d	(1,000)	9.050	1,350	2,450
Capital injection	10,000	–	–	–
Debtors	4,000	–	6,000	6,000
Sale of assets	–	200	–	–
	13,000	9,250	7,350	8,450
Creditors	3,000	4,000	4,000	14,000
Wages	500	500	500	500
General expenses*	450	400	400	400
Fixed Assets	–	3,000	–	–
Balance c/d	9,050	1,350	2,450	(6,450)

*See note 5. In November we pay $\frac{7}{8}$ of £400 for November and £100 outstanding from October = £450. In December we pay $\frac{7}{8}$ of £400 for December and $\frac{1}{8}$ of £400 for November = £400.

(c)   R. Norman: Forecast Trading, profit and loss account 4 months ending 28 February 1986

	£	£
Sales [Note 2]		37,500
Cost of goods sold [$\frac{2}{3}$ of sales]		25,000
Gross profit ($\frac{1}{3}$ of sales)		12,500
less Wages [Note 4]	2,000	
General expenses [Note 5]	1,600	
Rent [Note 6]	500	
Depreciation [Note 7] *	340	
Loss on disposal	440	4,880
Net profit		7,620

*Depreciation is 10 per cent p.a. on Assets at cost at end of February.

We have	£
Balance at cost b/d	8,000
add Purchases	3,000
	11,000
less Disposals at cost	800
	10,200

Four months' depreciation = $\frac{4}{12} \times 10\% \times £10,200 = £340$.

The disposal had been in existence for 2 years; its book value at time of disposal is £800 − 20% of £800 = £640. If it is sold for £200, there is a loss of £440.

16.6 Further exercise

Question 16.1

Alphasoft Ltd sell computer hardware and software. The company's summarised balance sheet as at 31 December 1984 was as follows:

	£		£
Authorised and Issued Capital		Fixed Assets	
40,000 £1 ordinary shares fully paid	40,000	Freehold property (market value as at	
Retained earnings as at 1 January 1984	75,000	1 July 1984 £120,000)	70,000
Net profit for year	45,000	Other fixed assets	32,000
Current liabilities	120,000	Current assets	
		Sundry assets	150,000
		Balance at bank	28,000
	280,000		280,000

The company had developed very rapidly and the directors decided to approach a bank for an overdraft in order to finance the sales of a new generation of micro-computers. The following forecast information was available for the first four months of the next financial year:

(1)

	Projected Unit Sales 1985			
	Jan.	Feb.	Mar.	Apr.
Old micros	30	40	30	35
New generation micros	70	90	100	140

In December 1984, 30 old micro-computers had been sold.

The old micro-computers were sold at £300 a unit, but from 1 March 1985 the old units were to be sold at £150 per unit in order to reduce stocks quickly. Cash arising from the sales was always received one month after the sale.

The new generation micro-computers were to be sold at £400 a unit and, in order to encourage sales, the period of credit to be allowed was extended to two months. No sales of new units had been made before 1 January 1985.

(2) Other Projected Sales Revenue

Currently, there were 150 maintenance contracts on units bought by customers at £300 a unit. Customers pay 10 per cent of the unit price annually, half on 1 February and half on 1 August.

No maintenance contracts would be available for the new generation of micro-computers.

Software sales generated £6,000 in the month of December 1984 and would be at the same level in January and February 1985. Thereafter software sales would earn £9,000 a month. All software sales receipts were received one month after sale.

(3) The gross profit-mark-up on all unit sales (old micros and new generation micros) is 25 per cent on cost.

(4) The old units were bought at the rate of 30 per month, but no purchases would be made after 31 January since existing stocks were to be cleared.

The new units had been bought at the rate of 100 per month since 1 October 1984 in order to build up stocks, and would continue at the rate of 100 a month in 1985.

Suppliers were always paid in the month following the purchase.

(5) Staff salaries were paid each month at £3,000 per month.

(6) Royalty payments were £500 a month payable quarterly in arrears commencing on 1 January each year.

(7) Other variable overhead was calculated at 5 per cent of each month's computer unit sales revenue only, and was always paid in the month following the sales.

(8) Fixed overhead costs were paid at £1,000 per month.

The company had requested a £40,000 overdraft and the bank replied asking for the information below.

REQUIRED

(a) The company's return on capital employed for 1984, based on the shareholders' interest as at 1 January 1984. No changes in issued capital or other revenue reserves had occurred during the year. *(1 mark)*

(b) A detailed cash budget for the four months ending 30 April 1985. *(14 marks)*

(c) A statement indicating the action taken by the company to obtain information in support of the projected sales figures for the new-generation machines and any other factors which might have been taken into account in making the projections. *(7 marks)*

(d) Indicate **two** ways in which the company could satisfy the bank's requirement for security for any overdraft facilities granted. *(3 marks)*

(AEB)

Answer 16.1

(a) ROCE = £45,000/£115,000 = 39.1%.

(b)

Alphasoft Ltd: Receipts schedule

	Jan. £	Feb. £	Mar. £	Apr. £
Debtors — old micros	9,000	9,000	12,000	4,500
Debtors — new micros	–	–	28,000	36,000
Maintenance receipts	–	2,250	–	–
Debtors — software	6,000	6,000	6,000	9,000
	15,000	17,250	46,000	49,500

Alphasoft Ltd: Payments schedule

	Jan. £	Feb. £	Mar. £	Apr. £
Creditors — old micros	7,200	7,200	–	–
Creditors — new micros	32,000	32,000	32,000	32,000
Staff salaries	3,000	3,000	3,000	3,000
Royalties	1,500	–	–	1,500
Variable overheads	450	1,850	2,400	2,225
Fixed overheads	1,000	1,000	1,000	1,000
	45,150	45,050	38,400	39,725

Alphasoft Ltd: Cash budget

	Jan. £	Feb. £	Mar. £	Apr. £
Opening balance	28,000	(2,150)	(29,950)	(22,350)
Receipts	15,000	17,250	46,000	49,500
	43,000	15,100	16,050	27,150
Payments	45,150	45,050	38,400	39,725
Closing balance	(2,150)	(29,950)	(22,350)	(12,575)

(c) Market research: indicating market growth, competition, acceptability + positioning of new product.

Other factors: continuity of supply; pattern of distribution; range of suitable software; quality of micros; back-up services; availability of peripheral devices.

(d) (1) Secure overdraft on freehold property or (2) a floating charge on fixed assets.

17 Variance Analysis

17.1 Introduction

Variance analysis is a means of comparing the firm's performance over a period against the budget for that period. Its purpose is to highlight areas of poor performance, known as adverse variances, as well as highlighting areas of 'good' performance, known as favourable variances.

Variance reports are usually produced on a monthly basis, so that attempts can be made by those responsible for the areas in which the variances occur to take corrective action. This is known as *management by exception.*

There are various methods of calculating variances. However, we suggest one particular style or format here, since we believe that it is the easiest one to remember.

Variance analysis compares the actual cost of, say, producing a unit, against how much it *should have* cost to produce a unit. How much it should have cost is known as the *standard cost.*

The cost of production consists of labour, materials, variable overheads and fixed overheads. Each of these items is analysed in detail. Any 'variation' from standard affects the actual profit for the period.

However, profit can also be affected by (a) the price the firm charges for the units sold, and (b) the actual quantity of units sold. Therefore, not only are cost variances important, but so also are sales variances.

17.2 Material variances

Material variances analyse (a) the actual costs of material used against standard cost of material used, and (b) the actual quantity of material used against the standard quantity of material used (for the output actually achieved). Let us look at a simple example.

Firm X	*Budget*	*Actual*
Production	1000 units	800 units
kg of raw material	200	175
Price per kg	£10	£10.20
Raw material cost	£2,000	£1,785

At first glance it appears that the firm has actually saved money against budget for raw materials, of £2,000 − £1,785 = £215. However, the firm had budgeted to produce 1,000 units, but it only produced 800. Therefore, it should have calculated how much it *should have spent* on raw materials for the 800 units actually produced. This is known as a *flexed budget*.

163

Flexed budget

kg Raw materials = (800/1,000) × 200 = 160 kg
Budgeted price per kg   £10

Budgeted raw material cost   £1,600

We should now compare the flexed budget with the actual results. This is done using the following format. In the examination you should set it out leaving at first an empty row between lines, as follows:

Actual quantity × actual price = £x
[empty row]
Actual quantity × standard price = £y
[empty row]
Standard quantity × standard price (for output achieved) = £z

The empty rows are then filled with the variances. The first empty row is the raw material price variance = £(y − x). The second empty row is the raw material usage variance = £(z − y).

Thus, for our example, we have:

Actual quantity × Actual price	= £1,785
Raw material price variance	£35 (A)dverse
Actual quantity × standard price	= £1,750
Raw material usage variance	£150 (A)dverse
Standard quantity × standard price	= £1,600

Both of the above variances are adverse, since the actual costs were greater than the standard costs.

17.3 Labour variances

Labour variances analyse (a) the wage-rate variance (i.e. how much the firm paid per hour of labour against the standard hourly rate, known as the 'labour rate' variance) and (b) how long it took labour to produce the output against how long it should have taken (i.e. the standard hours for the output achieved, known as the 'labour efficiency' variance).

Example

	Budget	Actual
Output	4,000 units	3,500 units
Labour	2,000 hours @ £5 = £10,000	1,900 hours at £4.75 = £9,025

We must first 'flex' the budget to 3,500 units:

Output	3,500 units
Labour	(3,500/4,000) × 2,000 hours @ £5 = £8,750

164

The labour for labour variances is very similar to that of the raw material variances

Actual hours at actual rate		£9,025
Labour rate variance		475 (F)avourable
Actual hours at standard rate [1,900 × £5]	=	£9,500
Labour efficiency variance		750 (A)
Standard hours × standard rate	=	£8,750

17.4 Variable overhead variances

Variable overheads are incurred usually in relation to the hours worked. Therefore, their variance analysis is very similar to that of the labour variances. The analysis format is as follows:

Actual hours worked × actual variable overhead hourly rate	£x
→ Variable overhead expenditure variance	£(y − x)
Actual hours worked × standard variable overhead hourly rate	£y
→ Variable overhead efficiency variance	£(z − y)
Standard hours × standard variable overhead hourly rate [for output achieved]	£z

17.5 Fixed overhead variances

Where a firm is using absorption costing for the valuation of finished goods, it includes in the valuation of those goods a certain proportion of fixed costs, based on (a) the budgeted fixed cost, divided by (b) the budgeted output. This is known as the 'standard absorption rate'. If the firm's actual volume of output is greater than budget, it would have charged out those goods with more than the budgeted fixed costs. It would have 'over-recovered' the budgeted fixed costs, otherwise known as a *favourable volume variance*.

Example

	Budget	Actual
Output	1,000 units	1,200 units
Fixed costs	£5,000	£5,600

The above example gives a standard absorption rate of £5 per unit (£5,000/1,000 units). Thus, we calculate the fixed overheads volume variance as follows:

Actual output at standard rate = 1,200 × £5	= £6,000	
→ Volume variance		£1,000(F)
Budgeted output at standard rate = 1,000 × £5	= £5,000	

Unlike previous variances, if the actual is greater than budget, we have a favourable volume variance.

(a) Fixed overhead expenditure variance

This is simply the difference between budgeted fixed overheads and actual fixed overheads. In the above example, we have

Budget £5,000
Actual £5,600

Fixed overheads expenditure variance 600 (A)

17.6 Sales variances

The layout for sales variances is similar to those for labour, materials and variable overheads.

Example

	Budget	Actual
Output/sales	4,000 units	4,800 units
price	£10	£8.50
Turnover	£40,000	£40,800

We look at the change to sales turnover caused by the difference in price, and the change to sales turnover caused by the change in volume. The format is as follows:

Actual volume at actual price	£40,800
→ Sales price variance	7,200 (A)
Actual volume at standard price	48,000
→ Sales volume variance	8,000 (F)
Budgeted volume at standard price	40,000

Notice that the price variance is adverse, because actual price is lower than standard, which has the effect of reducing profits, while the volume variance is favourable, since the firm sold more units than budget, which has the effect of increasing the firm's profits.

The *key format* for all variance analysis (except fixed overheads) which we have used is:

actual × actual

actual × standard

standard × standard

If you can remember this key format, you will find variance analysis quite simple.

17.7 Worked examples

Example 17.1

South Wales Refractories Ltd, manufacturers of special bricks for the steel industry, use a standard cost system. The following information was extracted from the firm's books for the month of March 1984:

	Budget for March	Actual Usage for March
Labour		
Direct Skilled Labour	400 hrs at £3.50 per hour	420 hrs at £3.80 per hour
Direct Unskilled Labour	800 hrs at £2.50 per hour	750 hrs at £2.60 per hour
Materials		
Steel	50 tons at £90 per ton	55 tons at £85 per ton
Chrome Ore	120 tons at £150 per ton	130 tons at £160 per ton

REQUIRED

(a) An explanation of the purpose of standard costing, including the factors which must be taken into account in setting standards. [*8 marks*]

(b) The standard and actual cost of production for the month of March. [*3 marks*]

(c) Calculate the following variances from standard:
   (i) direct wage rate variances;
   (ii) labour efficiency variances;
   (iii) material price variances;
   (iv) material usage variances. [*8 marks*]

(d) Comment on the material usage and material price variances calculated in (c), giving **one** possible reason for the variance in **each** case. [*6 marks*]

(AEB)

Solution 17.1

(a) The purpose of standard costing is to provide a quantified objective which various elements of management should try to adhere to — for example, production should attempt to achieve the standard hours, and no more than the standard hours, for each unit produced. Their performance will be measured against the standard, and any adverse variance will reflect on their success or failure in maintaining those standards.

    In setting standards, the areas of responsibility where those standards apply should have confidence in their ability in achieving those standards — i.e. the standards should not be viewed as 'unachievable' or else those areas of management will not even attempt to achieve those standards. On the other hand, the standards should not be seen as easily achievable, since this will not 'stretch' the capabilities of management. Therefore, a balanced or optimising standard should be set which is a challenge, drawing on the skills of management.

    Other factors, such as inflation, changes in technology, changes in production processes, should also be considered.

(b) This part simply looks at the aggregate figures given in the question.

	Budget		*Actual*	
	£	£	£	£
Skilled (400 × 3.5)	1,400		1,596	
Unskilled	2,000	3,400	1,950	3,546
Materials: Steel	4,500		4,675	
Chrome ore	18,000	22,500	20,800	25,475
		25,900		29,021

167

(c) If we lay out the variance analysis in the following format, the variances throw themselves out quite easily. Always attempt to use this technique in the examination. It is the easiest method I have found. (We shall find the variances for each type of labour, and for each type of material.)

Labour	Skilled	Unskilled
Actual hours × actual rate	420 × £3.8 = £1,596	750 × £2.6 = £1,950
→ Wage rate variance	£126(A)	£75(A)
Actual hours × standard rate	420 × £3.5 = £1,470	750 × £2.5 = £1,875
→ Labour efficiency variance	£70(A)	£125(F)
Standard hours × standard rate	400 × £3.5 = £1,400	800 × £2.5 = £2,000

Material	Steel	Chrome ore
Actual quantity × actual price	55 × £85 = £4,675	130 × £160 = £20,800
→ Material price variance	£275(F)	£1,300(A)
Actual quantity × standard price	55 × £90 = £4,950	130 × £150 = £19,500
→ Material usage variance	£450(A)	£1,500(A)
Standard quantity × standard price	50 × £90 = £4,500	120 × £150 = £18,000

Note: (A) = adverse; (F) = favourable.

(d) *Steel*   Here we have a favourable price variance of £275, but an adverse usage variance of £450. This could be due to the fact that the purchasing manager may have bought a cheaper but inferior quality of steel, with a resulting higher *wastage* factor.

Chrome ore   Here we have an adverse price *and* usage variance. Not only is the firm paying more for the chrome than standard, but also it is having to use more of it than standard. One possible reason for this may be general price increases in that commodity, coupled with a switch to an inferior grade of chrome ore in order to avoid even higher price increases.

Example 17.2

The management of Construction plc have asked for information on five of their current jobs. Among the information available is the following concerning the use of labour:

	Standard hours	Actual hours	Standard wage rate	Actual wage rate
Job No. 1.	150	142	£8	£8.50
2.	220	234	£7	£6.50
3.	50	48	£8	£8.40
4.	170	176	£8	£8.40
5.	140	140	£8.50	£8

The information concerning materials for the same jobs is:

	Standard price per metre	Actual price per metre	Standard use per unit	Actual use per unit
Job No. 1.	£19	£21	500	482
2.	£22	£18	410	450
3.	£18	£17	300	290
4.	£21	£22	180	190
5.	£20	£18	150	180

You are required to prepare notes to form the basis of a report to management on your findings for the five jobs.
The report will ultimately contain:

(a) The total actual cost of each job,   [5]
(b) The net or total variance for each job,   [5]
(c) The labour efficiency and rate variances for each job where the labour variance is adverse, and the material usage and price variances for each job where the material variance is adverse,   [20]
(d) An indication to management of the order in which the variances shown in (b) and (c) should be investigated, giving reasons why,   [5]
(e) Suggestions of possible causes for the good or bad performances.   [5]

(OLE)

Solution 17.2

This is a long, but not difficult question. Care must be taken in part (c) of the question, where variances are required *only* for particular jobs. Some thought should be given to the layout of the answer.

Actual costs

(a) Job no.	1	2	3	4	5
	£	£	£	£	£
Labour [hours × rate]	1,207*	1,521	403.20	1,478.40	1,120
Materials [metres × price]	10,122†	8,100	4,930.00	4,180.00	3,240
Total	11,329	9,621	5,333.20	5,658.40	4,360

*142 hours at £8.50 per hour.
†482 metres at £21 per metre.

Standard costs

Job No.	1	2	3	4	5
	£	£	£	£	£
Labour	1,200	1,540	400	1,360	1,190
Materials	9,500	9,020	5,400	3,780	3,000
Total	10,700	10,560	5,800	5,140	4,190

(b) ### Variances

	£	£	£	£	£
Labour variance	(7)	19	(3.20)	(118.40)	70
Materials	(622)	920	470	(400)	(240)
Net variance	(629)	939	466.8	(518.40)	(170)

Parentheses indicate
adverse variances

169

(c) The jobs where labour variances are adverse are Nos. 1, 3 and 4. With careful thought given to layout we have:

Job No.

	1 £	3 £	4 £
Actual hours × actual rate	1,207	403.20	1,478.40
→ Labour rate variance	71(A)	19.2(A)	70.4(A)
Actual hours × standard rate	1,136	384	1,408
→ Labour efficiency variance	64(F)	16 (F)	48 (A)
Standard hours × standard rate	1,200	400	1,360

The jobs where material variances are adverse are Nos. 1, 4 and 5.

Job No.

	1 £	4 £	5 £
Actual quantity × actual price	10,122	4,180	3,240
→ Material price variance	964(A)	190(A)	360(F)
Actual quantity × standard price	9,158	3,990	3,600
→ Material usage variance	342(F)	210(A)	600(A)
Standard quantity × standard price	9,500	3,780	3,000

(d) We should begin by looking at those jobs with overall adverse net variances — i.e. Job No. 1 has a net variance of £629(A), which, as a percent of its standard cost, is $(629/10,700) \times 100 = 5.9$ per cent. Job No. 5 has a net variance of £170(A), which is 4.1 per cent over the standard cost.

Therefore, we should investigate Job No. 1 and then Job No. 4. After these, we should look at other adverse variances by labour or materials, and assign an order of priority to largest percentage relative variances.

(e) Possible causes for good performances:
overestimation of standard job costs;
employment of more efficient labour;
use of higher-quality materials.

Possible causes for bad performances:

underestimation of standard job costs;
increase in negotiated wage rates;
high wastage of materials.

17.8 Further exercise

Question 17.1

Perriwinkle Ltd manufacture and sell a single product and the following summarised information represents the original forecast profit budget and the subsequent actual results for the year ended 30 April 1986.

	Budget £		Actual £
Sales (Selling price £15 per unit)	105,000	(Selling price £13.50 per unit)	101,250
Direct materials	21,000		23,000
Direct labour	14,000		16,000
Variable manufacturing overhead	10,500		11,000
Fixed manufacturing overhead	16,000		18,000
Gross profit	43,500		33,250
Variable sales overhead	7,000		8,000
Other fixed costs	12,000		12,000
Net profit	24,500		13,250

Additional information.

(1) The company had prepared the profit budget on the basis that 7,000 units would be produced and sold. The number of units actually sold during the year was 7,500.
(2) No stocks of finished goods were held and there was no work in progress.

Note: It should be assumed that all expense and revenue relationships remain unchanged except where specifically identified.

REQUIRED

(a) Calculate the budget volume of sales units necessary to achieve the budget break-even point in 1985/86. [4 marks]
(b) Calculate the volume of sales units to achieve the actual break-even point. [4 marks]
(c) Prepare a break-even chart to illustrate the budgeted and actual sales/costs relationships for 1985/86. Identify the break-even points. [8 marks]
(d) Calculate the sales variance for 1985/86, distinguishing between the sales price variance and the sales volume variance. [5 marks]
(e) Briefly outline the limitations of break-even analysis. [4 marks]

(AEB)

Answer 17.1

Although this question is mainly concerned with break-even analysis (see Chapter 14), part (d) question is concerned with sales variances. However, here is the full solution.

(a) Budget break-even in units, using the formula

$$\text{break-even units} = \frac{\text{budgeted fixed costs}}{\text{budgeted contribution}}$$

Budgeted fixed costs = manufacturing overhead £16,000 + 'other fixed costs' £12,000

$$= £28,000$$

Budgeted contribution = budgeted price £15 − budgeted variable costs per unit

		£
Budgeted variable costs =	materials	21,000
	labour	14,000
	variable manufacturing	10,500
	variable sales	7,000
		52,500

171

Budgeted variable costs per unit $\dfrac{52,500}{\text{budgeted output}} = \dfrac{52,500}{7,000} = £7.50$

∴ Budgeted contribution = price £15 − variable cost £7.50 = £7.50

∴ Budgeted break-even = $\dfrac{£28,000}{£7.50} = 3,733$ units

(b) Actual break-even = $\dfrac{\text{actual fixed costs}}{\text{actual contribution}} = \dfrac{£30,000}{\text{actual contribution}}$

Actual contribution

$= £13.50 - \dfrac{£(23,000 + 16,000 + 11,000 + 8,000)}{7,500}$

$= £13.50 - £7.73 = £5.77$

Break-even $= \dfrac{30,000}{5.77} = 5,199$ units

(c) Periwinkle Ltd: Break-even chart

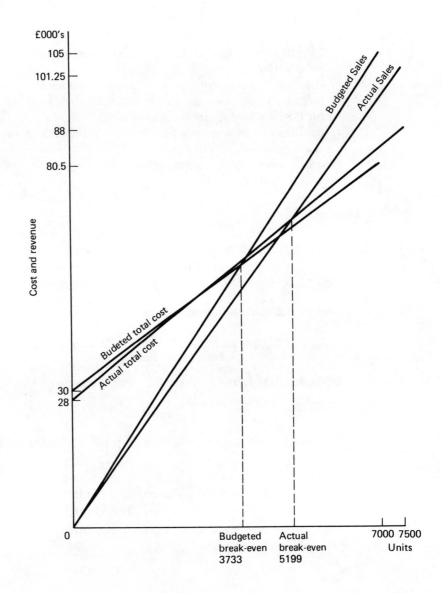

172

(d) Here we can use the format for sales variances as given in the text (Section 17.6).

Actual volume at actual price = 7,500 × £13.5 = £101,250

→ Sales price variance   £ 11,250(A)

Actual volume at standard price = 7,500 × £15 = £112,500

→ Sales volume variance   7,500(F)

Budgeted volume at standard price = 7,000 × 15 = 105,000

(e) Limitations of break-even:
   (i) assumes linear relationships;
  (ii) does not clearly show profit/loss at different levels of output.

18 Ratio Analysis

18.1 Introduction

Ratio analysis is a numerical attempt to analyse the performance and financial position of a business. By converting absolute numbers into ratios, we have the ability to make comparisons between one firm and another, or between one period and another. Indeed, ratio analysis, which is the interpretation of ratios, cannot be meaningfully achieved without some form of comparison.

For example, if a firm's gross profit/sales margin is 60 per cent, we cannot say whether this is 'high' or 'low' or 'good' or 'bad', without considering (a) the gross margin of its competitors and (b) its gross margin last year and in previous years.

In the following sections we shall have a look at the 'key ratios'. When answering examination questions where you are asked to comment on ratios, the golden rule is to state only the obvious. Do not start to make assumptions for which you have no data.

18.2 Pyramid of ratios

The pyramid of ratios is a technique used to analyse a firm's profitability and efficiency, but remember that commentary can only be made if we have enough data for comparisons, either between two firms (known as *static* comparisons) or between two periods (known as *dynamic* comparisons).

The basic pyramid of ratios looks like this:

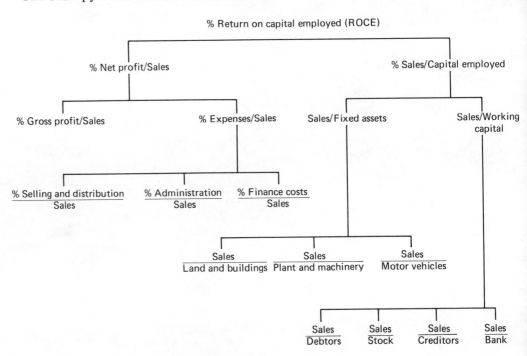

By using this pyramid, as illustrated in Worked Example 18.1, we can gradually and systematically track down the causes of any adverse performance, and eventually make suggestions as to where management may be able to take action in order to bring about improvements in the future.

Return on capital employed (ROCE) can be calculated by several methods. The most common method is net profit/owner's capital + long-term liabilities × (100/1).

From here we branch left and right. The left-hand side of the pyramid highlights pricing (gross margin) and expenses relative to turnover (level of activity). The right-hand side highlights the efficiency in terms of use of resources – e.g. for every £ of plant machinery, how many £s' worth of turnover was generated?

In the working capital section of the pyramid we have some crude ratios, which are here to indicate some possible problem areas. They should be calculated more accurately if we are provided with sufficient data.

(i) Sales/debtors or debtors turnover ratio should really be calculated as credit sales/average debtors. The result can then be divided into 12 for months' or 365 for days' credit given. For example, a debtors turnover of 10 means that the firm is giving 12/10 = 1.2 months' credit or 365/10 = 36.5 days' credit.

(ii) Sales/stock or stock turnover should really be calculated as cost of goods sold/average stock.

(iii) Sales/creditors shows how many £s' worth of turnover was achieved for every £s' worth of credit taken. However, we should also calculate the creditors turn, which is credit purchases/average creditors and show how frequently the firm pays off its creditors.

18.3 Liquidity ratios

Liquidity ratios are designed to assess the firm's relative ability to meet its short-term debts.

The most significant liquidity ratio, also known as the *acid test* is current assets less stock/current liabilities and shows the clearance, if any, which the firm has in terms of liquid or near-liquid assets over immediate debts. Many textbooks suggest that this ratio should ideally be no less than 1:1; however, many firms are able to operate successfully on a ratio of less than 1:1, since they have a rapid stock turnover and little or no credit sales (e.g. Sainsbury).

The other ratio which is also a test of 'solvency' is the working capital ratio or 'current ratio' (current assets/current liabilities). If this ratio were less than 1:1, it would indicate a negative amount of working capital (current assets − current liabilities). A trading company could find itself in serious difficulties, since it would be unable to pay its ongoing operational expenses, *and* be able to pay off its creditors.

On the other hand, working capital can be at too high a level. An overinvestment in stock, debtors or cash can imply idle resources which might be used more profitably if transferred to a more long-term investment such as plant or buildings, which can be used to generate production and/or sales.

18.4 Investors' ratios

In this section we shall look at those ratios of interest to shareholders or potential shareholders of limited companies, apart from the ratios already mentioned.

(i) $\% \text{ Dividend} = \dfrac{\text{dividend (in pence) per share}}{\text{nominal value per share}} \times \dfrac{100}{1}$

where nominal value is the 'face' value of the share, *not the market value*.

(ii) $\% \text{ Yield} = \dfrac{\text{dividend per share}}{\text{market value per share}} \times \dfrac{100}{1}$

This formula reflects the return, in terms of income, on the current market value of the shareholder's investment.

(iii) $\text{Dividend cover} = \dfrac{\text{net profit after tax} - \text{preference share dividends}}{\text{interim} + \text{final dividend}}$

This formula is a reflection of the 'dividend policy' of the firm. It shows how many times over the firm could have paid the dividends it actually paid. A high cover, say 10, indicates that the firm is retaining 90 per cent of its profits in the business, while a cover of, say, 2 indicates that it is returning 50 per cent of its profits.

(iv) $\text{Earnings per share (EPS)} = \dfrac{\text{net profit after tax} - \text{preference dividends}}{\text{number of issued ordinary shares}}$

This formula signifies how much each ordinary share has earned in terms of profits, and is not affected by dividends.

$$\text{Price/earnings (P/E) ratio} = \dfrac{\text{market price per share}}{\text{EPS}}$$

This ratio has become increasingly popular recently with financial analysts. Technically it is interpreted as how many years it would take for each share to earn its current market value, if earnings continued at the current level. However, it is really used as a reflection of the market's confidence in the future performance of the company. Many shares of plcs have P/E ratios in the 10–20 range; however, a glance at the financial press will reveal a range from less than 5.0 to more than 90.

18.5 Gearing

Gearing has become a popular topic with examiners. It is a way of looking at the long-term financial structure of a business, in terms of the ratio between fixed-interest capital (such as long-term loans, debentures and preference shares) and equity capital (issued share capital and reserves).

There are two ways of expressing the gearing:

(i) The gearing ratio is easily remembered as $G = F/E$, where G = gearing, F = fixed interest borrowing (including preference shares) and E = equity. Thus, a firm with £100,000 of loan capital, £50,000 of issued preference shares and £300,000 issued share capital + reserves can be said to have a gearing ratio of 1.5:3 or 1:2.

(ii) A second way of expressing gearing is as a percentage:

$$\%G = \frac{F}{F + E} \times \frac{100}{1}$$

In the above example, the gearing is $(150,000/450,000) \times (100/1) = 33$ per cent, which means that 33 per cent of the firm's long-term capital is in the form of fixed interest of fixed dividend certificates.

High gearing (i.e. where at least 50 per cent of the capital is fixed interest) is said to be 'high-risk' structure, for the simple reason that the ordinary shareholder is unlikely to achieve any earnings in periods of 'low profits', owing to relatively high amounts of interest and preference dividends that will have to be paid before there is any amount left over for the ordinary shares. On the other hand, when profits are high, and because of the relatively low number of ordinary shares in a high-geared company, the earning per share will be greater than if the firm had been low-geared (see Worked Example 18.2).

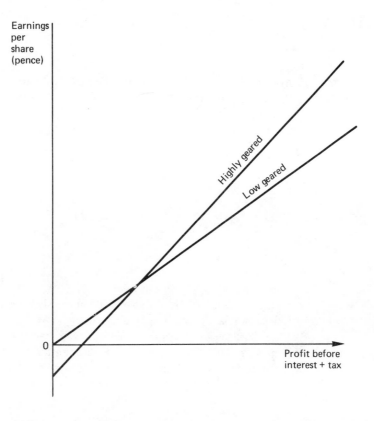

The relationship between earnings and gearing is best illustrated by a diagram. As can be seen, high-geared = greater risk, but possibly much greater returns to the (ordinary) shareholder.

18.6 Worked examples

Example 18.1

Martha is the accountant of a trading business. During the past year she produced interim accounts for the six months ended 30 November 1985, and draft final accounts for the year ended 31 May 1986, as follows:

	Interim Accounts £	Draft Final Accounts £
Sales (all on credit terms)	140,000	336,000
Cost of sales (note 1)	42,000	112,000
Gross profit	98,000	224,000
Less expenses	56,000	168,000
Net profit	42,000	56,000
Fixed assets	70,000	63,000
Current assets (note 2)	42,000	71,000
Current liabilities (note 3)	(22,000)	(30,000)
	90,000	104,000
Share capital	30,000	30,000
Retained earnings	60,000	74,000
	90,000	104,000

Notes

1. Average stock was £14,000 during the first six months.
2. Current assets were:

	30 *November* 1985 £	31 *May* 1986 £
Stock	16,000	25,000
Debtors	24,000	28,000
Bank	2,000	18,000
	42,000	71,000

3. Current liabilities consisted entirely of trade creditors.

Martha informs you that the business leased additional premises from 1 December 1985, and that sales arising therefrom totalled £70,000 for the six months to 31 May 1986, with an average mark-up on cost prices of 150 per cent being made on those goods.

Expenses relating to these additional premises totalled £21,000 for the period. Two-fifths of the closing stock of the business was located at these premises.

Prepare a report, using appropriate accounting ratios, to explain the changes in the financial situation of the business during the year ended 31 May 1986. [*15 marks*]

(London)

Solution 18.1

In order to explain any changes, we should compare the first six months' performance against that of the second six months. Therefore, we must calculate the second six months' profit and loss by deducting the respective first six months' profit and loss figures from the final profit and loss.

Thus, we have:

Profit and loss: 6 months ended 31 May 1986

	£000s
Sales	196
Cost of sales	70
Gross profit	126
Expenses	112
Net profit	14

We can now construct a pyramid of ratios; the first six months' figures are in parentheses.

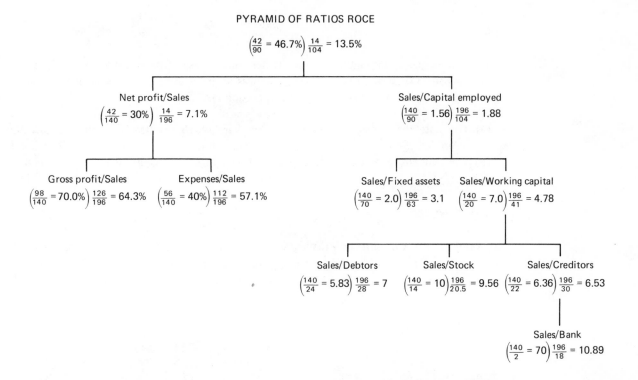

PYRAMID OF RATIOS ROCE

$\left(\frac{42}{90} = 46.7\%\right) \frac{14}{104} = 13.5\%$

Net profit/Sales
$\left(\frac{42}{140} = 30\%\right) \frac{14}{196} = 7.1\%$

Sales/Capital employed
$\left(\frac{140}{90} = 1.56\right) \frac{196}{104} = 1.88$

Gross profit/Sales
$\left(\frac{98}{140} = 70.0\%\right) \frac{126}{196} = 64.3\%$

Expenses/Sales
$\left(\frac{56}{140} = 40\%\right) \frac{112}{196} = 57.1\%$

Sales/Fixed assets
$\left(\frac{140}{70} = 2.0\right) \frac{196}{63} = 3.1$

Sales/Working capital
$\left(\frac{140}{20} = 7.0\right) \frac{196}{41} = 4.78$

Sales/Debtors
$\left(\frac{140}{24} = 5.83\right) \frac{196}{28} = 7$

Sales/Stock
$\left(\frac{140}{14} = 10\right) \frac{196}{20.5} = 9.56$

Sales/Creditors
$\left(\frac{140}{22} = 6.36\right) \frac{196}{30} = 6.53$

Sales/Bank
$\left(\frac{140}{2} = 70\right) \frac{196}{18} = 10.89$

From the above calculations, we can see that the return on capital employed was only 13.5 per cent in the second six months, compared with 46.7 per cent in the first six months. This was mainly due to the relatively high level of expenses in the second six months, which were 57.1 per cent of sales, compared with only 40 per cent of sales in the first six months.

In terms of use of assets, we generated more sales per £ of fixed assets (at book value) in the second period, but this is only to be expected, owing to depreciation.

We have more than doubled our investment in working capital, from £20,000 at the end of November to £41,000 at the end of May. However, we seem to have a relatively high bank balance. This could be reduced, and used for investment in fixed assets.

If the business had not leased the additional premises, sales for the second six months would have been £126,000, yielding a gross profit of £126,000 − ($\frac{3}{5}$ × £70,000) = £84,000, a gross margin of 67 per cent.

The expenses of the business would have been £112,000 − £21,000 = £91,000, and the net profits would have been £84,000 − £91,000 = −£7,000 (a loss!).

179

Our conclusion is that expenses in the older part of the business have dramatically increased. If the new site had not been leased, then the firm would have made a loss in the second six months.

Recommendation   Reduce expenses in established site as a priority. Second, investigate alternative investments, rather than have excess funds in the bank.

Example 18.2

Three companies have the capital structures shown below.

Company	A	B	C
	£000s	£000s	£000s
Ordinary shares	600	400	50
12% Debentures	–	200	550
	600	600	600

The return on capital employed was 20 per cent for each firm in 1984, and in 1985 was 10 per cent. Corporation tax in both years was assumed to be 55 per cent, and debenture interest is an allowable expense against corporation tax.

(a) Calculate the percentage return on the shareholders' capital for each company for 1984 and 1985. Assume that all profits are distributed.   [*17 marks*]
(b) Use your answer to explain the merits and the dangers of high gearing.   [*8 marks*]
(London)

Solution 18.2

(a) The return on capital employed is measured before interest + tax. We can calculate (i) profit before interest and tax, and then (ii) net profit after tax. Finally, we can express this as a percentage of shareholders' capital.

Company	A		B		C	
	1984	1985	1984	1985	1984	1985
	£000s	£000s	£000s	£000s	£000s	£000s
Profit before interest and tax	120	60	120	60	120	60
Interest	–	–	24	24	66	66
net Profit before tax	120	60	96	36	54	(6)
Tax	66	33	52.8	19.8	29.7	–
Net Profit after tax	54	27	43.2	16.2	24.3	(6)
Ordinary share capital	600	600	400	400	50	50
% Return on shareholders' capital	9	4.5	10.8	4.1	48.6	(12)

(b) Company C is the most highly geared of the three companies, with a gearing ratio of 11:1. One of the merits of being highly geared is the relative high return to ordinary shareholders when profits are high. In this example, C returns 48.6 per cent, while A returns only 9 per cent. However, in a highly geared firm, the return on shareholders' capital or earnings per share (EPS) is much more volatile than in a low-geared company. Notice how for shareholders in Company A their return falls by 4.5 percentage points when profits fall, but for company C shareholders their return falls from 48.6 per cent to −12 percent, a fall of 60.6 percentage points, even though the reduction in profits before interest and tax is the same for both companies.

See also Further Exercise 19.1.

18.7 Further exercises

Question 18.1

The following financial information relates to two businesses in the same line of business for the year ended 30 April 1984:

	A. Fresco's Business			B. Pick's Business	
£	£		£	£	
	420,000	Sales	250,000		
	50,000	Average stock at cost	80,000		
	16,000	Drawings for theyear	21,500		
	15,000	Selling and administration expenses	25,000		
	20%	Gross Profit margin on cost	25%		
	£	Balance Sheets as at 30 April 1984	£		
		Fixed Assets			
	—	Land and Buildings (At cost)	100,000		
	60,000	Plant and machinery (Net book value)	55,000		
	25,000	Motor vehicles (Net book value)	28,000		
	85,000			183,000	
		Current assets			
30,000		Stock	60,000		
70,000		Trade debtors	35,000		
20,000		Balance at bank	—		
5,000	125,000	Cash	1,500	96,500	
	210,000			279,500	
		Financed by:			
	181,000	Capital account		203,500	
		Current liabilities			
28,000		Trade creditors	46,000		
1,000		Accrued expenses	2,000		
—	29,000	Bank overdraft	28,000	76,000	
	210,000			279,500	

Notes:
(1) During the year Fresco had bought a motor vehicle for private use but it had been treated as a business vehicle. The cost of the vehicle was £10,000 and it had been depreciated by £2,500.
(2) Pick's works manager advised him that stock bought on 1 September 1983 for £10,000, and included in the closing stock, was redundant and of no value. Pick decided to write off the stock; no entries had yet been made.
(3) Fresco owned the business's land and buildings but they had not previously been brought into account. His accountant advised him to record them in the business's books on a retrospective basis. The land and buildings were valued at £118,000 on 1 May 1983.

N.B. Ignore depreciation on land and buildings.

(a) After making all the necessary adjustments for each separate business calculate:
  (i) the rate of stock turnover;
  (ii) the gross profit/sales and the net profit/sales ratios;
  (iii) the working capital ratio;
  (iv) the return on proprietor's capital employed calculated on the adjusted opening capital. [*14 marks*]
(b) As a potential buyer of one of the businesses, draft a short report indicating which business appears to be the more attractive investment. Include in your report any reservations you may have and use the results of your calculations to support your argument. [*11 marks*]
(AEB)

Answer 18.1

(a) (i) Rate of stock turnover = $\dfrac{\text{cost of goods sold}}{\text{average stock}}$

We are not told the cost of goods sold, but we can calculate it, since we are given sales and gross profit 'margin' on cost.

For Fresco, the gross profit/cost = 20 per cent. Therefore, sales (cost + profit) = 120 per cent of cost.

$$\therefore \text{Cost} = \frac{100}{120} \times \text{sales} = \frac{100}{120} \times £420{,}000 = £350{,}000$$

Therefore,

Fresco's rate of stock turnover = $\dfrac{350{,}000}{50{,}000} = 7$ p.a.

Similarly,

Pick's cost of sales = $\dfrac{100}{125} \times \text{sales} = \dfrac{100}{125} \times £250{,}000$

$$= £200{,}000$$

Note 2 does *not* affect Pick's average stock holding, therefore,

rate of stock turnover = $\dfrac{200{,}000}{80{,}000} = 2.5$ p.a.

(ii) Gross profit/sales for Fresco is determined by his gross profit/cost margin. If this, which is normally called a percentage mark-up, is 20 per cent or $\frac{1}{5}$, then gross profit/sales = $1/(5 + 1) = \frac{1}{6}$ or $16\frac{2}{3}$ per cent.

For Pick, we must make an adjustment for the reduction in value of stock of £10,000 (note 2). If we ignore this at first, Pick's gross profit would have been $\frac{1}{5}$ of sales (£250,000) = £50,000, but, because of the reduction in stock value, the gross profit is now reduced to £40,000, giving us a gross profit/sales ratio of $(40/250) \times (100/1) = 16$ per cent.

To calculate the net profit/sales percentage, we need to calculate net profit!

	Fresco	Pick
	£	£
Gross profit	70,000	40,000
less Selling + administration expenses	(15,000)	(25,000)
add back Depreciation on private motor	2,500	–
Net profit	57,500	15,000
Sales	420,000	250,000
Net profit/sales	13.7%	6%

(iii) Working capital ratio = current assets/current liabilities

	Fresco	Pick
	£	£
Current assets	125,000	96,500 – 10,000 stock = 86,500
Current liabilities	29,000	76,000
Working capital ratio	4.31:1	1.14:1

(iv) The return on the proprietor's adjusted opening capital is given by the formula

$$\text{net profit}/(\text{closing capital} - \text{net profit} + \text{drawings}) \times \frac{100}{1}$$

	Fresco	Pick
	£	£
Closing capital	181,000	203,500
less Net profit (unadjusted)	55,000	25,000
	126,000	178,500
add Book drawings	16,000	21,500
	142,000	200,000
Fixed asset adj.	118,000	–
Opening capital	260,000	200,000

We must now use the corrected net profit to calculate the return.

	Fresco	Pick
	£	£
Net profit	57,500	15,000
Opening capital	260,000	200,000
% return on capital	22.1%	7.5%

Note that there is no need to adjust Fresco's capital for the motor vehicle. It was treated as a business asset, and we assume was paid for from the business bank account.

(b) On the basis of the above calculations, Fresco is a far more attractive investment than Pick. The return on capital for Fresco is nearly 3 times greater than that of Pick. Fresco is able to earn a greater net profit/sales margin, owing to his relatively low overheads, even though Fresco's turnover is £420,000, compared with Pick's £250,000. However, I would suggest that Fresco should attempt to reduce his level of working capital. The ratio of 4.31:1 is far too high. He could perhaps reduce his debtors, since he is giving them an average of two months' credit ([70/420] × [12/1]).

Question 18.2

How does 'stock turn' differ from 'turnover'? What is the importance of stock turn in ratio analysis and how is it calculated?

Answer 18.2

Stock turn is the rate at which stock is replaced or turned over during a period (usually a year), whereas *turnover* is the level of sales achieved during a period.

Stock turn is an important ratio, since it is an indication of how efficient the firm is in the area of *stock control*. If stock turn is relatively low, it indicates that the firm is holding on average too high a level of stock for the volume of trade achieved. If stock turn is relatively high, it indicates rapid replacement of stock and here the firm may find that it has, on occasion, been 'out-of-stock' on various products.

The stock turn ratio is calculated as follows:

$$\frac{\text{cost of goods sold in the period}}{\text{average stock held in the period}}$$

Usually we are only given information on opening and closing stocks, in which case the average stock is simply

$$\frac{\text{opening stock} + \text{closing stock}}{2}$$

If, say, the stock turn for a year's trade is 6, this means that the firm is, on average, replacing stock once every two months (12 months/6).

19 Funds Flow Statements

19.1 Introduction

The purpose of the funds flow statements is to show the movement of funds into and out of the firm for the period (year). In particular, it highlights the size of the increase or decrease in working capital for that period, and what has caused that increase or decrease.

A change in the amount of working capital can only be caused by changes in other sections of the balance sheet. The composition of working capital can change (e.g. less stock and more debtors), but the actual amount of working capital can only change if the total sources of finance (profits, capital, disposal of fixed assets, long-term loans, etc.) is not the same as the total application of funds (purchase of fixed assets, repayments of loans, payment of dividends, payment of tax, etc.)

If the source of funds are greater than the application of funds, this must result in an increase in working capital.

Example: A simplified balance sheet (£000s)

Sundry Fixed assets	£12	
Current assets	8	
Current liabilities	6	
Working capital		2
Total assets less current liabilities		14
Long-term loans		5
Net worth		9
Financed by capital + reserves		9

Suppose that the following happens in the next financial year

(i) Net profit for year	£3
(ii) Increase in share capital	4
(iii) Purchases fixed assets	2

(We shall ignore depreciation for the moment)

The net profit results in a flow of funds into the firm (sales less cost of goods sold and expenses). Even if the sales were all on credit and still not realised, this will increase our current asset of debtors.

The increase in share capital results in a flow of cash into the firm.

The purchase of fixed assets results in a flow of cash out of the firm, or, if they were bought on short-term credit, must result in a decrease in working capital (current assets less current liabilities).

Therefore, by examining these sources and applications of funds, we can determine their net effect on working capital.

Source of Funds

Net profit for year	£3
Increase in share capital	4
Total sources	7
Applications	
Purchase of Fixed assets	2
net Increase in Working capital	5

We can then go on to examine the changes that have taken place to each element of working capital and show that in fact the net effect of all these changes (increase/decrease in stock, debtors, creditors, bank) explains the overall change in working capital.

The funds flow statement's main purpose is to explain how a business obtains and uses its funds, and indicates whether a business is generating enough funds to meet its needs or whether it is approaching insolvency.

19.2 SSAP10

SSAP10 provides the following format for a source and application of funds statement.

Source and Application of Funds for year ended 198X

Net profit before tax			£X
Adjustments for items not involving the movement of funds			
depreciation for the year		£X	
(Profit) or Loss on disposal of fixed assets		(£X) or £X	
Increase or (decrease) in provision for doubtful debts		£X or (£X)	£X
Funds generated from operations			X
Funds from other sources			
Proceeds from sale of fixed assets		£X	
Sales of investments		X	
Issue of share capital		X	
New loans/debentures		X	X
Total source of funds			X
Application of funds			
Dividends paid		£(X)	
Tax paid		(X)	
Purchase of fixed assets		(X)	
Repayment of loans		(X)	
Redemption of shares		(X)	X
Increase/(decrease) in working capital			£X or (X)
Movements of working capital			
Increase/(decrease) in stock		£X or (X)	
Increase/(decrease) in debtors		£X or (X)	
Decrease/(increase) in creditors		£X or (X)	
Movement in net liquid funds			
Increase/(decrease) in bank	£X or (X)		
Increase/(decrease) in cash	£X or (X)		
Increase/(decrease) in short-term investments	£X or (X)	£X or (X)	£X or (X)

There are some technical points arising from the above statement.

The adjustments section is there because certain charges made against net profit are not movements of cash, and therefore must be taken into account when arriving at the figure for 'funds generated from operations'.

In the 'application of funds' section, we have 'dividends paid'. This means the actual monies paid to shareholders as dividends during the year. It will be the sum of last year's proposed dividends (which are paid during this year) and this year's interim dividend. It must not include any proposed dividends at the end of this year, since they have not been paid by the end of this year.

The 'tax paid', which is also in the application section, is similar in its treatment to dividends. We show only the tax paid during this year, and we must not include any tax provision made against this year's profits.

19.3 Worked example

Question 19.1

The summarised balance sheets of Maxin Ltd at 31 October 1984 and 1985 are as follows:

	1984		1985	
	£	£	£	£
Fixed Assets				
Freehold property, at valuation		50,000		50,000
Fixtures and fittings, at cost	40,000		60,000	
Less aggregate depreciation	(24,000)	16,000	30,000	30,000
		66,000		80,000
Investments at cost		7,000		11,000
Current assets				
Stocks	5,000		14,000	
Debtors	8,000		6,000	
Balance at bank	4,000		7,000	
		17,000		27,000
		90,000		118,000
Issued capital				
£1 ordinary shares fully paid		50,000		70,000
Reserves				
Share premium		12,000		20,000
Retained earnings		6,000		8,000
Current liabilities				
Creditors	14,000		16,000	
Proposed dividends	8,000		4,000	
		22,000		20,000
		90,000		118,000

Notes
(1) There have been no disposals of fixture and fittings during the year ended 31 October 1985.
(2) An interim dividend for the year ended 31 October 1985 of £5,000 was paid during the year.

A sources and applications of funds statement for the year ended 31 October 1985, showing the change in working capital over that year. [*16 marks*]

(AEB)

Solution 19.1

This is a very straightforward funds flow question.

Source and Application of Funds for year ended 31 October 1985

Sources of funds	£	£
Net profit for year [Working 1]		11,000
Adjustments for items not involving the movement of funds:		
Depreciation for year		6,000
Funds generated from operations		17,000
Funds from other sources:		
Issue of ordinary shares [Working 2]		28,000
Total sources		45,000
Application of funds		
Purchase of fixtures	20,000	
Purchase of investments	4,000	
Payment of dividends [Working 3]	13,000	
Total applications		37,000
Increase in working capital		8,000
Movements in working capital		
Increase in stock	9,000	
Decrease in debtors	(2,000)	
Increase in creditors	(2,000)	5,000
Movements in net liquid funds:		
Increase in bank		3,000
		8,000

WORKING 1	£
Net profit for year =	
increase in retained earnings	2,000
interim dividends during year	5,000
proposed dividends at end of year	4,000
	11,000

		WORKING 2		£

WORKING 2	£
Increase in fully paid ordinary shares	20,000
Increase in share premium	8,000
Shares issued for	28,000

WORKING 3	£
Dividends paid =	
last year's proposed dividends	8,000
add Interim dividends paid	5,000
	13,000

19.4 Further exercises

Question 19.1

Bill Waddy, a shareholder owning 10,000 shares in Maplex Ltd., received the following summarised financial information for the years ended 31 December 1982 and 31 December 1983:

Balance Sheet as at 31 December

1982 £	1982 £		1983 £	1983 £
		Fixed Assets (at Net book value)		
60,000		Freehold land and property		180,000
65,000		Plant and machinery (Net book value)		85,000
	125,000			265,000
	50,000	Investments (at cost)		57,000
		Current Assets		
55,000		Stocks	115,000	
43,000		Trade debtors	74,000	
18,000		Cash	3,000	
116,000			192,000	
		Less Current Liabilities £		
20,000		Trade creditors 26,000		
10,000		Proposed dividend 15,000		
20,000		Bank overdraft 60,000		
50,000	66,000		101,000	91,000
	241,000			413,000
		Financed by:		
		Share Capital		
	100,000	£1 Ordinary shares fully paid		100,000
		Reserves		
	45,000	Share premium		45,000
		Land revaluation		120,000
	65,000	Retained earnings		117,000
	210,000			382,000
		Loan Capital		
	31,000	10% Debentures 1983–86		31,000
	241,000			413,000

Profit and Loss Appropriation account for the year
ended 31 December 1983

	£	£
Net profit after tax		75,000
less Net dividends		
Interim (paid)	8,000	
Final (proposed)	15,000	23,000
Transferred to retained earnings		52,000

Notes:

(1) There was a revaluation of the freehold land and property in 1983 but there were no purchases or sales of property. It is company policy not to provide for depreciation on freehold property.

(2) The depreciation on plant and machinery was £17,000 for the year and there were no revaluations or sales of plant and machinery.

(3) There have been no sales of investments during the year.

(4) The net profit before dividends was £69,000 for the year ended 31 December 1982.

Bill was a very worried man since a friend told him that the company had proposed a rights issue because the company had liquidity problems and the company's profitability was down. The rights issue was made on 1 January 1984 on a one for one basis at £1.25 a share. The proceeds of the issue had been used to redeem the outstanding debentures at par and the remainder to reduce the bank overdraft.

REQUIRED

As Bill's adviser, prepare the following statements:

(i) a sources and applications of funds statement for the year ended 31 December 1983 showing the change in working capital over the year;   [12 marks]

(ii) an explanation to Bill of how the rights issue had improved the liquidity position and a calculation of the bank balance on 1 January 1984.   [6 marks]

(AEB)

(continued opposite)

Answer 19.1

(ai)

Source and Application of Funds for year ended 31 December 1983

Sources of Funds	£	£
Net profit for year	75,000	
Adjustments:		
Depreciation plant and machinery	17,000	
Funds generated from operations		92,000
Funds from other sources		−
Total sources		92,000
Application of Funds		
Purchase of plant	37,000	
Payments of dividends	18,000	
Purchase of investments	7,000	62,000
Increase in working capital		30,000
Movements in Working Capital		
Increase in stock	60,000	
Increase in debtors	31,000	
Increase in creditors	(6,000)	85,000
Movement in net liquid funds		
Increase in overdraft	(40,000)	
Decrease in cash	(15,000)	(55,000)
		30,000

(aii) A rights issue is an issue of shares to existing shareholders, for cash. In Bill's case the issue is on a basis of one new share for existing issued share. There are 100,000 existing ordinary shares; then there were 100,000 new shares issued at £1.25 − 9.e. £125,000. The bank calculation is as follows:

Opening balance (overdraft)	(£60,000)
Rights issue	£125,000
Closing balance	£65,000

Question 19.2

The following information is available from Whiteacres plc:

(a)

1983 £	Balances as at 31 December	1984 £
1,652,000	Turnover for the year	1,437,600
972,400	Cost of sales	845,200
1,100,000	Issued 10% Redeemable preference shares £1 each	900,000
920,000	Issued Ordinary shares £1 each	1,220,000
184,000	Share premium	58,000
56,000	Other revenue reserves	66,000
1,969,200	Fixed assets at book value	1,988,000
84,200	Stock	73,600
97,280	Trade debtors	192,280
109,160	Bank (debit balance)	29,060
254,840	Creditors	233,440
120,000	9% Debenture stock	84,000
450,000	Investments — long-term	420,000
75,000	Profit and loss account	141,500

(b)
 (i) Included in the administration costs and the distribution costs for 1984 was depreciation of fixed assets £46,300 and £26,900, respectively.
 (ii) Creditors include dividends proposed of £202,000 for 1983 and £187,600 for 1984.
 (iii) During 1984 investments were sold at a profit of £5,000, which has been deducted from the administration costs for the year.
 (iv) At 1 January 1983 there was a provision for doubtful debts of £6,400. This provision was reduced in December 1983 to £5,120 and was increased in December 1984 to 5 per cent of the debtors. The debtors shown in the accounts are net of this provision.
 (v) In May 1984 a bonus issue of shares was made of 2 new £1 Ordinary shares for every 10 held.
 (vi) New £1 ordinary shares had been issued at a premium of 50p each in October 1984.
 (vii) No fixed assets had been sold during the year.

You are required to:

Prepare a Funds Flow Statement for the year ending 31 December 1984 showing clearly the change in working capital.

(OLE)

Answer 19.2

We must first calculate the net profit for the year. The way to do this is to look at the change in retained profits, reserves and dividends. Thus we have

	£	£
Increase in Profit and loss a/c balance	141,500	
	−75,000	66,500
Increase in revenue reserves	66,000	
	−56,000	10,000
Proposed dividends 1984 =		187,600
net profit for year		264,100

We can now draft the funds flow statement.

Whiteacres plc:— Funds Flow Statement year ended 31 December 1984

	£	£
Net profit for year		264,100
Adjustments		
add Depreciation for year	73,200	
deduct Profit on sale of investments	(5,000)	
add Increase in provision for doubtful debts [Working 1]	5,000	73,200
Funds generated from operations		337,300
Funds from other sources:		
Sale of investments [Working 2]	35,000	
Issue of shares for cash [Working 3]	174,000	209,000
Total sources		546,300
Application of funds		
Redemption of preference shares	200,000	
Purchase of fixed assets [Working 4]	92,000	
Payment of dividends	202,000	
Redemption of debentures	36,000	530,000
Increase in working capital		16,300
Movements in working capital		
Reduction in stock	(10,600)	
Increase in debtors [Working 5]	100,000	
Decrease in creditors [Working 6]	7,000	96,400
Movements in net liquid funds		
Decrease in bank		(80,100)
		16,300

WORKING 1: Provision for doubtful debts	£
Provision at end of 1984 = £192,280 × (5/95) =	10,120
Provision at start of 1984 =	5,120
∴ Increase in provision	5,000

WORKING 2 £

Reduction in investment = £450,000 − £420,000 =	30,000
add Profit on sale	5,000
Sales value	35,000

WORKING 3 £

Ordinary share capital 31 December 1984 =	1,220,000
less Opening balance	920,000
	300,000
less Bonus issue [(2/10) × 920,000]	184,000
Issue of shares cash (116,000 @ £1.50)	£174,000

WORKING 4: Purchase of fixed assets £

Opening balance	1,969,200
less Depreciation for year	73,200
Balance without purchases	1,896,000
Closing balance	1,988,000
∴ Purchases =	92,000

WORKING 5 £

Gross debtors end 1983 = £97,280 + provision £5,120 =	102,400
Gross debtors end 1984 = £192,280 × (100/95) =	202,400
Increase in debtors	100,000

WORKING 6 £

Trade creditors 31/12/1983 = Total creditors	254,840
less proposed dividends	202,000
	52,840
Trade creditors 31/12/1984 = Total creditors	233,440
less proposed dividends	187,600
	45,840
Decrease in creditors (£52,840 − £45,840) =	7,000

20 Capital Budgeting

20.1 Introduction

Capital budgeting is really about how the firm decides which fixed assets are a 'worthwhile' investment or which alternative investments are the most profitable or financially attractive. There are four techniques commonly used:

  (i) The average rate of return
 (ii) Payback
(iii) Net present value (NPV)
(iv) Percentage yield or internal rate of return (IRR)

None of these methods needs to be used in isolation. Quite often management will evaluate investment projects using two or more of the above investment appraisal techniques.

20.2 The average rate of return

This method simply looks at the average annual profit earned by a project, and expresses this average profit as a percentage of the original cost of the investment, taking into account any scrap or disposal value at the end of the project's life.

Example

A machine costs £10,000, and shows a net cash inflow for five years of £3,500 p.a. Its scrap value at the end of year 5 is estimated at £400. The average rate of return is therefore

$$\frac{\text{average profit}}{\text{cost}} = \frac{(5 \times 3,500 + 400 - 10,000)/5}{10,000}$$

$$\frac{1,580}{10,000} = 15.8\%$$

By adding back the scrap value and deducting the original cost, we are, in fact, taking into account depreciation in the calculation of the average rate of return.

20.3 Payback

This method looks at how long, in terms of cash flow, it will take for the project to recover its original cost. The calculation often involves parts of years. It assumes that cash is received evenly through each year. From the example used above, we can build up the cumulative cash flow for the end of each year.

	£
end year 1	3,500
year 2	7,000
year 3	10,500
year 4	14,000
year 5	17,500

We can see that the £10,000 original cost is recovered at some point after the end of year 2, but before the end of year 3. Assuming an even cash flow during year 3, the fraction of year 3 that needs to expire before the £10,000 total is achieved is given by

$$\frac{£10{,}000 - \text{year 2 cumulative total}}{\text{year 3 cash flow}} = \frac{10{,}000 - 7{,}000}{3{,}500} = 0.86$$

Therefore, the payback period for this project will be 2.86 years. Obviously, the shorter the payback period, the more attractive the investment project.

The major criticism of this technique is that it ignores any cash flows beyond the payback point in time. Thus we could have 2 projects, both with the same payback, but one earns £100,000 beyond payback, and the other only £1,000, yet both would be given equal praise under the payback system.

20.4 Net present value (NPV)

The NPV method takes into consideration the cash flows of the whole life of the investment project, and also considers the 'time value' of money.

This takes into consideration the fact that most people would rather have £1 now than £1 in five years' time, since £1 in five years' time will be worth considerably less than £1 now, owing mainly to (a) inflation and (b) the rate of interest, or 'opportunity cost' of money.

The NPV method takes into account the time value of money by 'discounting' further cash flows to an equivalent present value. This is achieved by (a) choosing a percentage discount rate, and (b) using the net present value tables, which are found in books of statistical tables. Here is an extract:

Discount rate	16%	18%	20%
end year 1	0.862	0.847	0.833
end year 2	0.743	0.718	0.694
end year 3	0.641	0.609	0.579
end year 4	0.552	0.516	0.482

From the table we can determine that if the firm uses a discount rate of 18 per cent, then £1 received at the end of year 3 will only be worth 60.9 p (its present value).

The method of calculating the NPV of a stream of cash flows is simply a matter of adding together the discounted values of each year's cash flow.

For example: A machine costs £25,000, and generates the following net cash inflows:

year 1 £7,000, year 2 £10,000, year 3 £12,000, year 4 £14,000

The company uses a 16 per cent discount rate.

We call the time of the original investment year 0. Thus, we have the following:

	(1) Cash flow	(2) 16% Discount rate	(1) × (2) Discounted cash flow
	£		£
Year 0	−25,000	1.0	−25,000
Year 1	7,000	0.862	6,034
Year 2	10,000	0.743	7,430
Year 3	12,000	0.641	7,692
Year 4	14,000	0.552	7,728
			NPV 3,884

The NPV of £3,884 is positive and the project is therefore worth while. Notice that the year 0 discount factor is always 1.0.

20.5 Percentage yield or internal rate of return (IRR)

This method of capital investment appraisal has an advantage over the NPV method in that it does not use an assumed (subjective) discount rate, but instead calculates the discount rate which would result in the net present value of discounted cash flows being zero. Once the IRR has been determined, it can be compared with the firm's objective or target rate of return, and the project can be accepted or rejected on that criterion.

The IRR is found by trial and error. Select a discount rate. Calculate the NPV for the project. If this NPV is positive, it implies that the selected discount rate was too low. Select a higher discount rate, until the resulting NPV is negative. The IRR will be between these last two selected discount rates; its value can be found by estimation, using linear proportions.

For example, for a project a 10 per cent discount rate gives a NPV of £500, and a 12 per cent discount rate gives a NPV of −£100. Therefore, the IRR can be estimated by the formula 10% + [(500/600) × 2%] = 11.6%
or by drawing a graph.

20.6 Worked examples

Example 20.1

(a) Explain the relationship between Net Present Value (NPV) and Yield (Internal Rate of Return). [*4 marks*]
(b) A firm is considering an investment project costing £12,500. The estimated annual cash flows accruing at the end of each year are:

Year 1	£2,500	Year 3	£5,700
Year 2	£4,600	Year 4	£7,000

If the company has to borrow money to finance the project, is the maximum rate of interest it should pay for finance: 16%? 18%? 20%? Give reasons for your answer.

Table of factors

Period	16%	18%	20%
1	0.862	0.847	0.833
2	0.743	0.718	0.694
3	0.641	0.609	0.579
4	0.552	0.516	0.482

[*11 marks*]
(L)

Solution 20.1

(a) Net present value (NPV) is the aggregate of a series of annual cash flows which have been discounted using an assumed discount rate. The result can be a positive or negative value. However, the yield or internal rate of return is the percentage discount rate which would result in a series of discounted cash flows having an aggregate value of zero.

(b) What we have to do here is discount the cash flows and calculate their net present values, using the 16 per cent, 18 per cent and 20 per cent discount rates. If the NPV is negative, the rate of interest is too high.

		Discount rate					
		16%		18%		20%	
	Cash flow	Factor	DCF	Factor	DCF	Factor	DCF
	£		£		£		£
Year 0	−12,500	1.0	−12,500	1.0	−12,500	1.0	−12,500
Year 1	2,500	0.862	2,155	0.847	2,118	0.833	2,083
Year 2	4,600	0.743	3,418	0.718	3,303	0.694	3,192
Year 3	5,700	0.641	3,654	0.609	3,471	0.579	3,300
Year 4	7,000	0.552	3,864	0.516	3,612	0.482	3,374
		NPV	+ 591		+ 4		− 551

The maximum rate of interest the company should pay for finance is 18 per cent, since this yields a net present value of almost zero. Any rate of interest above 18 per cent will yield a negative net present value.

Example 20.2

Ambergate Ltd decided to employ a management consultant to advise on the purchase of a new machine for its factory. Three different machines were being considered for purchase and the company accountant provided the consultant with the following information:

	Machine N £	Machine P £	Machine Q £
Cost	24,000	26,500	16,800
Estimated			
Net cash inflows			
Year 1	4,000	8,000	6,000
Year 2	6,500	10,000	7,000
Year 3	10,000	9,000	7,000
Year 4	9,000	6,500	6,000
Year 5	2,000	3,000	6,000
Year 6	1,500	1,000	5,000

Additional information

(1) The firm selling machine N was prepared to buy the machine back at the end of the fourth year for £4,000.
(2) Machines N and P would have no scrap value at the end of the sixth year.
(3) Machine Q had an expected life of only three years (nil scrap value), at the end of which an identical machine would have to be purchased, cost £18,000.
(4) The rate of interest applicable to the transaction was 12 per cent per annum.
(5) The following is an extract from the present value table for £1:

12%

Year 1 0.893
Year 2 0.797
Year 3 0.712
Year 4 0.636
Year 5 0.567
Year 6 0.507

(6) All net cash inflows arise at the end of the relevant year.

REQUIRED

(a) Evaluate the purchase of each separate machine by the
    (i) pay back method (in years to two places of decimals);
    (ii) net present value method.   [15 marks]
(b) As the consultant, write a report for Ambergate advising which specific machine should be purchased. Indicate any reservations that you may have regarding the methods used to evaluate this capital project.   [10 marks]

(AEB)

Solution 20.2

(a)

(i) Payback method:

	Machine N £	Machine P £	Machine Q £
Cost	24,000	26,500	16,800 + 18,000 year 3
Cumulative inflow			
Year 1	4,000	8,000	6,000
Year 2	10,500	18,000	13,000
Year 3	20,500	27,000	20,000
Year 4	29,500	33,500	26,000
Year 5	31,500	36,500	32,000
Year 6	33,000	37,500	37,000

The payback is measured in terms of how long it takes for the cumulative cash inflow to equal that of the original cost.

$$\text{Machine N payback} = 3 \text{ years} + \frac{24,000 - 20,500}{9,000 \ [\text{year 4 inflow}]} = 3.39 \text{ years}$$

$$\text{Machine P payback} = 2 \text{ years} + \frac{26,500 - 18,000}{9,000 \ [\text{year 3 inflow}]} = 2.94 \text{ years}$$

Machine Q payback: here we can take the two separate outflows together; therefore, a total outflow of £34,800.

$$\text{Payback} = 5 \text{ years} + \frac{34,800 - 32,000}{5,000 \ [\text{year 6 inflow}]} = 5.56 \text{ years}$$

Therefore, by the payback criterion, machine P is the more attractive investment.

(ii) Net present value method:

	Discount factor	*MACHINE N* Cash flow £	DCF £	*MACHINE P* Cash flow £	DCF £	*MACHINE Q* Cash flow £	DCF £
Year 0	1.0	−24,000	−24,000	−26,500	−26,500	−16,800	−16,800
End Year 1	0.893	4,000	3,572	8,000	7,144	6,000	5,358
Year 2	0.797	6,500	5,181	10,000	7,970	7,000	5,579
Year 3	0.712	10,000	7,120	9,000	6,408	7,000 − 18,000	−7,832
Year 4	0.636	9,000	5,724	6,500	4,134	6,000	3,816
Year 5	0.567	2,000	1,134	3,000	1,701	6,000	3,402
Year 6	0.507	1,500	761	1,000	507	5,000	2,535
Net present value			−£ 508		£1,364		−£3,942

(b) Report: Ambergate Capital Investment Appraisal

On the basis of two evaluation methods required, it appears that machine P is the most attractive choice, in terms of both payback and net present value.

Machine P pays back after 2.94 years, machine N after 3.39 years, and machine Q after 5.56 years.

In terms of NPV, investment in machine P yields an NPV of £1,364, in machine N −£508, and in machine Q −£3,942.

The payback method of appraisal has one major weakness: it ignores any cash flow beyond the payback point in time, as well as ignoring the 'time value' of money.

The net present value method hasn't these problems, but its major weakness is the choice of the percentage discount rate. How can the firm be sure that the 12 per cent discount rate will be an accurate discount rate for the next 6 years?

20.7 Further exercise

Question 10.2

Moray Ferries Ltd own a single ship which provides a short sea ferry service for passengers, private vehicles and commercial traffic. The present ship is nearing the end of its useful life and the company is considering the purchase of a new ship.

The forecast operating budgets using the present ship are as follows:

	1986 £M	1987 £M	1988 £M	1989 £M	1990 £M
Estimated Revenue Receipts					
Private traffic	2	3	4.5	6	7
Commercial traffic	3	4	4.5	5	6
	5	7	9.0	11	13
Estimated Operating Payments	4	5	6.5	7.5	9
	1	2	2.5	3.5	4

The ships being considered as a replacement are as described below.

(1) Ship A   Cost £10M

This ship is of similar capacity to the one being replaced, but being a more modern ship it is expected that extra business would be attracted from competitors. It is anticipated therefore that estimated revenue receipts would be 10 per cent higher in each year of the present forecast.

There would be no change in operating payments.

(2) Ship B   Cost £14M

This modern ship has a carrying capacity 30 per cent greater than the present ship. It is expected that private traffic receipts would increase by £$\frac{1}{2}$M a year in each year of the forecast. Commercial traffic receipts are expected to increase by 15 per cent in each of the first two years and by 30 per cent in each of the remaining years.

Operating payments would increase by 20 per cent in each year of the forecast.

Additional information.

(3) The company's cost of capital is 15 per cent per annum.
(4) It is company policy to assume that ships have a life of 20 years.
(5) It should be assumed that all costs are paid and revenues received at the end of each year.
(6) The following is an extract from the present value table for £1:

	12%	14%	15%	16%
Year 1	£0.893	£0.877	£0.870	£0.862
Year 2	£0.797	£0.769	£0.756	£0.743
Year 3	£0.712	£0.675	£0.658	£0.641
Year 4	£0.636	£0.592	£0.572	£0.552
Year 5	£0.567	£0.519	£0.497	£0.476

(7) All calculations should be made correct to 3 places of decimals.

REQUIRED

(a) Revised operating budgets for 1986–1990 for each of the alternatives being considered.

[*7 marks*]

(b) Appropriate computations using the net present value method for **each** of the ships, A and B.

[*8 marks*]

(c) A report providing a recommendation to the management of Moray Ferries Ltd as to which course of action should be followed. Your report should include any reservation that you may have.

[*10 marks*]

(AEB)

Answer 20.1

(a)

Ship A: Forecast operating budget

	1986 £m	1987 £m	1988 £m	1989 £m	1990 £m
Estimated Revenue	5.5	7.7	9.9	12.1	14.3
Existing operating payments	4	5	6.5	7.5	9.0
Operating profit	1.5	2.7	3.4	4.6	5.3

Ship B: Forecast operating budget

	£m	£m	£m	£m	£m
Private traffic	2.5	3.5	5.0	6.5	7.5
Commercial traffic	3.45	4.6	5.85	6.5	7.8
	5.95	8.1	10.85	13.0	15.3
Operating payments	4.8	6.0	7.8	9.0	10.8
Operating profit	1.15	2.1	3.05	4.0	4.5

(b)

	Ship A Operating profits	Discount factor	Present value	*Ship B* Operating profit	Present value
	£m		£m	£m	£m
Year 1	1.5	0.870	1.305	1.15	1.001
2	2.7	0.756	2.041	2.1	1.588
3	3.4	0.658	2.237	3.05	2.007
4	4.6	0.572	2.631	4.0	2.288
5	5.3	0.497	2.634	4.5	2.237
		DCF	10.848		9.121
less Capital outflow			10.000	less Capital outflow	14.000
		NPV	0.848	NPV	−4.879

(c) From the above calculations, it is obvious that ship A is the more attractive purchase. In fact, ship B results in a negative net present value – i.e. cost of capital is greater than operating profits when discounted.

Reservations:

1. Scrap values of ships at end of 20 years?
2. How accurate are revenue projections?
3. If ship A is same size, will we be able to increase traffic?
4. What is current value of present ship profits?

21 Use of Computers in Accounting

21.1 Introduction

We cannot attempt here to provide a full authoritative text on the use of computers in accounting, but merely an outline of their applications, along with a few definitions and some suggested answers to typical examination questions.

21.2 Applications

Applications fall into two main areas.

(i) *Financial accounting*   Computers and electronic data processing can be used to replace the mundane aspects of a 'book-keeper's' work or 'writing up' the books of accounts. He can, after training, use a suite of computer accounting programs or 'packages' to do this for him. There are 'off the shelf' (pre-written) items of accounting software available to process accounting data.

Many of these accounting packages are 'modular'. This means that a fully integrated computerised accounting system can be built up gradually. This has advantages in terms of cash outflow and flexibility for the smaller businesses. The firm can first buy, say, a sales ledger system, to handle its customer accounts, invoicing, statements, etc., and at a later stage expand the system by adding the payroll module to handle its wages and salaries processing, to produce the payslips, printed cheques, etc. Other modules can be added later – e.g. purchase ledger, nominal ledger and cash book. Once the full system is installed, the firm can be provided with profit and loss statements and balance sheets as frequently as required by the use of a few commands.

(ii) *Management accounting*   In the area of analysis and decision-making, the availability of up-to-date information is invaluable. Thus, immediate access to the latest profit and loss statements has its advantages. In addition, more specialised programs can be used to aid decision-making. For example, computers can be used to generate frequent 'variance' reports, so that action can be taken quickly to reverse adverse results.

One particular type of software which management and management accountants find extremely valuable is known as a 'spreadsheet'. Many brands are available as off-the-shelf packages for micro-computers; among the best-known are Lotus 1–2–3, Visicalc, Supercalc. A spreadsheet is simply a large area of rows and columns, made up from a collection of addressable cells; the spreadsheet is like a grid. Each cell on the grid has a reference number or grid number. Text, numbers or formulas can be entered (via the keyboard) into any of the cells, and arithmetic and statistical operations performed on the contents of the cells. Management can use spreadsheets for a whole variety of needs, but the most common applications are budgeting, forecasting and statistical analysis of results.

There are many benefits to using spreadsheets, but the biggest advantage is that of 'what if?' calculations – i.e. what if raw material costs increase by 5 per cent, 10 per cent or 15 per cent. How will this affect our budgeted profit? By using a spreadsheet, immediate implications of changes to relevant figures can be seen on the VDU and, if required, printed out on a report.

More recently, computer graphics have become added features of spreadsheets, so that charts can be printed of, say, budgeted monthly sales and profits, for inclusion in management reports.

Note: For the larger computer systems (mainframes) as opposed to the desk-top or 'stand-alone' micros, specialist, tailor-made software is written to suit the firm's individual needs or systems, but the smaller firm, with, say, one or two micros will often find it more economical to buy the 'off-the-shelf' software.

21.3 Worked examples

Example 21.1

Give simple definitions of hardware and software in a computer configuration. Give two examples of each that could be used in a computerised accounting system.

(OLE)

Solution 21.1

The hardware in a computer system is the physical part of the system, such as keyboards, VDUs, processing unit, printers, etc., while software is defined as the programs or sets of instructions given to the computer telling it what operations to perform and how to perform them.

Two examples of hardware in the computerised accounting system would be:

1. The keyboard to input the accounting data such as credit sales transactions.
2. The VDU to display the details of a debtors account.

Two examples of software would be:

1. A payroll program to perform wage calculations, deductions, etc., and produce payslips.
2. A sales ledger program to produce invoices, statements, etc., for debtors.

Example 21.2

How does the information in a 'transaction file' differ from that in a 'master file'. Include in your answer examples of such information in a typical accounting computer run.

(OLE)

Solution 21.2

Files are simply areas of stored data. The data used in accounting, like any other data, need to be classified or put into some sensible and usable order.

Transaction files hold transaction data. There will be a transaction for sales. When a transaction (a sale) takes place, it is added to the transaction file, and will be deleted from the file after the transaction has been processed.

A master file holds standing data – that is, data which are used over and over again (e.g. data on customers, such as their name, account number, address, etc.).

Thus, on a typical accounting run data will be taken from the sales transaction file (i.e. sales of goods to customers); they will then be compared with information on the master file to ensure that valid data on customers have been entered in the transaction file, and, once cleared, sales will be recorded in the customer file and an invoice generated.

Example 21.3

What is a posting run in a computer accounting system? Give two examples of such runs and explain what information is being posted. (OLE)

Solution 21.3

A posting run is the processing of data from a transaction file so that the relevant records can be updated. Examples would be:

1. A Sale to Solid State Ltd is held on the transaction file. When the processing run takes place, the details of this sale are added to Solid State's account and its balance increased accordingly, and the stock figure reduced accordingly.
2. When the firm makes a series of payments to its creditors, the posting run will make appropriate entries in the purchases ledger.

Example 21.4

(a) Write a brief report to the owners of a business, identifying the advantages that a computerised system would bring to the accounting functions of the business, distinguishing between:
  (i) the clerical aspects of accounting;
  (ii) the management accounting function.
(b) State three limitations of a computerised accounting system.

Solution 21.4

(a)

Report: *Computerised Accounting System*

Clerical Accounting

Advantages A computerised system would enable clerical staff to become significantly more involved in their tasks, since their work could be reorganised to a more 'whole task' approach – i.e. instead of just concentrating on sales data, or invoices or credit control, or receipts, they could become responsible for a whole group of customers and be responsible for all transactions, rather than just a small portion. This would be likely to improve motivation. There will also be the obvious advantage of automatic rather than manual or calculator-based, calculations.

Advantages Almost instantaneous access to accounting information, either on paper or VDU, with the added advantage of 'what if?' calculations on alternatives open to management.

(b) Three Limitations
    (i) It can only process the data it is fed. Therefore, there is always the problem of 'rubbish in — rubbish out'.
    (ii) Future changes in the business usually imply expensive modifications to software and/or additions to hardware.
    (iii) A breakdown in the equipment can leave management stranded, without essential information on which to base decisions.

Index